57 Scientifically-Proven Survival Foods to Stockpile

How to Maximize Your Health with Everyday Shelf-Stable Grocery Store Foods, Bulk Foods, And Superfoods

by Damian Brindle

===> Get dozens of free survival guides, hundreds of videos, 600+ "how to" articles, gear reviews and so much more here: https://rethinksurvival.com

Disclaimer

The material covered within is for informational purposes only. I take no responsibility for what you do with this knowledge and I cannot be held responsible for any property or medical damages caused by the items or information you read about within. I would advise you to check your local laws as it's possible that some of the items or advice I offer may be illegal in some areas, and I would highly advise you against their use in said areas. Moreover, by using any information or material found within, you assume all risks for the material covered. You agree to indemnify, hold harmless, and defend the author, Damian Brindle, from all claims and damages arising from the use, possession, or consequences of the information covered. By taking and/or using any informational resources found within, you agree that you will use this information in a safe and legal manner, consistent with all applicable laws, safety rules, and good common sense. You further agree that you will take such steps as may be reasonably necessary or required by applicable law to keep any information out of the hands of minors as well as untrained and/or irresponsible individuals.

Table of Contents

Introduction

This book is intended to provide useful, actionable survival strategies as quickly as possible. As such, it's written to be fast to read and includes few product images as well as minimal tables.

Regarding Website Links

Realize, too, that this was originally written to be an electronic book only with many website links referenced throughout. Because this is a paperback book, however, referencing these links can be tedious if you had to type them into your web browser by hand. To make this easier on you, I have consolidated all referenced links into a single resource here: https://rethinksurvival.com/books/food-links.html.

When new links are introduced, they will be referenced with superscripts which will then correspond to the appropriate URL on the above referenced website page.

For completeness, however, all referenced links will also be included in Appendix B.

Grab Your Free 57-Point Checklist

Odds are that you won't remember all the foods discussed when you're done reading this book. To make your life easier, I've created a free, easy-to-reference, 57-point foods to stockpile checklist you can download that highlights everything discussed. You'll find a link to it here so that you can follow along if you like as well as at the end of this book in Appendix A, but please do read the entire book first. Now, download your free, easy-to-reference survival foods to stockpile checklist here.[1]

Prepare Yourself for Disaster in Only 5 Minutes

Since you clearly understand the need to prepare yourself, I want to share with you my unique 5 Minute Survival Blueprint, from which you'll discover just how to keep your family safe and secure from disasters of all kinds in only 5 minutes a day quickly, easily, and inexpensively.[2]

More Survival Books You'll Enjoy

If you liked what you read when finished, you can find more survival and preparedness books I've written at https://rethinksurvival.com/kindle-books/.[3]

This Book's Tone

As noted before, this book is written in a quick, simple, easy-to-read format. Hence, it is presented in a conversational form and not one that is intended to be grammatically correct. Getting you and your family ready for emergencies is the sole focus of this book.

And My Thanks

I also want to thank those folks who took the time to review this book, to offer their own suggestions, and to correct my mistakes. You know who you are.

Where You Should Start

When most people first contemplate preparing themselves for disaster, they usually think of one thing—food. There's obviously good reason for their natural focus on food since we literally need it to survive. With that in mind, and because I know you want to get the most out of your prepping dollar, we will look at food with a more clinical view than most preppers probably would. Specifically, we're going to seek out foods which maximize their usefulness in your survival when food may be scarce.

This advice is a bit different than what I usually tell people to do, which is to get started with prepping their pantry by simply purchasing more of the shelf-stable foods they already eat. After all, there's a lot of sense to this strategy since you already enjoy these foods, know how to cook with them, and it's likely that you instinctively include a variety of foods to choose from as it is. Chances are good, therefore, that you'll be well served with doing just that.

Nevertheless, if you want to get the most out of your survival pantry when times get tough, then we need a better plan. To do so, we're going to attempt to build out a well-stocked pantry by focusing on the nutritional aspects of foods, that is, by selecting foods which maximize stuff our bodies need, such as vitamins, minerals, fats, and so on, rather than only purchasing foods that we're accustomed to eating.

As an example, if you had to choose between eating a stalk of celery or a broccoli floret, which would you choose to eat assuming you want to maximize nutrients? That's easy to answer since nutritionally speaking the broccoli wins hands-down. While this may be somewhat instinctive, science tells us without a doubt that broccoli is loaded with vitamins and plenty more calories than an equivalent amount of celery.

And that's what we're going to do here, find those foods which maximize their nutritional benefit to us if we're unable to resupply or to purchase foods we normally rely upon for this purpose, particularly fresh foods, such as meats, dairy, vegetables, and fruits.

Note: Be aware that I'm not a healthcare professional of any sort and that the recommendations herein may not suit your unique needs or health concerns. Please do consult a knowledgeable healthcare provider or nutritional consultant if you have any special dietary requirements that may not be considered in this book or if the advice given is contrary to advice already given.

What a Healthy Diet Should Include

Before we get too far ahead of ourselves, we need to ask a crucial question: What does the body need to maximize health? Sadly, the answer isn't as straightforward as I would like it to be. You see, the body has many needs from food, not only to stay alive but also to remain healthy.

For starters, and with regards to staying healthy, the body needs a wide variety of vitamins and minerals— the key being a wide variety—and no doubt most folks understand that. With regards to staying alive, the body needs thousands of calories each day, and most folks understand this as well.

Beyond the basics mentioned above, we also need macronutrients—literally defined as substances needed in large amounts by living organisms—which include carbohydrates, fats, protein, and fiber. Let's briefly discuss each of these needs now.

Vitamins and Minerals

The major vitamins you need include Vitamins A, C, D, E, K, as well as an assortment of B vitamins, and choline (not to be confused with chlorine for water treatment).

The major minerals include calcium, chromium, copper, fluoride, iodine, iron, magnesium, manganese, molybdenum, phosphorus, selenium, zinc, potassium, sodium, and chloride (also not to be confused with chlorine or choline).

To keep things a bit less cluttered, here's a reference PDF file on vitamin and mineral intake levels based on age.[4]

Carbohydrates

Carbohydrates tend to get a bad rap at times but they're a must-consume nutrient because the body literally breaks them down and converts them into simple sugars which we use for energy. The good news is that most foods contain carbohydrates, so we don't have to try very hard to get them. There is a difference in the type of carbohydrates—either simple or complex—but we'll leave these details alone for the purposes of this book.

Fats

Fats, like carbohydrates, also get a bad rap but, again, nothing could be further from the truth. Your body needs fats. Repeat this with me: Fats are good! Well, the right kinds of fats and in relative moderation, of course.

In fact, I've been told that you need at least three tablespoons of fat in your diet daily to keep your joints working well, to keep hair [from] breaking off, and fingernails from breaking vertically. However, foods with fat have a lesser shelf life because the fat goes rancid.

Sadly, most Americans get too much of the wrong type of fats, specifically saturated fats (e.g., butter, lard) and trans fats, such as those found in shortenings and in many crackers and cookies, for instance. When it comes to survival, though, fats are fats (with the exception of trans fats which increase your risk of developing heart disease and stroke and type 2 diabetes), in my opinion, and we should tend toward foods that contain more fat rather than less unless you have some very specific dietary reason not to consume them.

Protein

Protein is another vital macronutrient. In fact, protein is considered the building block of life. That obviously means protein is important. More specifically, it's the amino acids—categorized as essential, nonessential, and conditional—that are the building blocks which make up protein and are, therefore, critical to our body's health.

There does seem to be some controversy as to whether one must eat animal sources of protein or not. The consensus seems to be generally not, but with some caveats. Regardless of where you get your protein from, the important part to remember is that the body cannot make essential amino acids, these you must get from food. Nonessential amino acids, on the other hand, the body can make.

Last, conditional amino acids often found in meat, dairy, seeds, nuts, and beans usually aren't considered necessary but may become so during times of stress and illness; disasters, accordingly, are an ideal time for needing these amino acids.

Fiber

Last, but not least, is fiber. There are two kinds of fiber, soluble and insoluble, both of which are necessary in a healthy diet. Fiber adds bulk to your diet, aids with digestion, helps prevent constipation, and more. A healthy diet needs fiber as well, but usually not too much.

Macronutrients: How Much Do You Need?

The answer invariably depends on age as well as other factors, such as being pregnant, but, in general, here's what the average adult male and female need daily:

	Male	Female
Calories	2000-3000*	1600-2400*
Carbohydrates	130 grams	130 grams
Total Fats	20-35 grams	25-35 grams
Protein	71 grams	46 grams
Fiber	30-38 grams	21-25 grams

*Depends on age and activity level. See this reference for details.[5]

With Regards to Children

Children's needs vary widely depending on age and, to be honest, I'm hesitant to put firm numbers on their dietary needs in this book for the simple fact that I feel children should be allowed to eat as much food as they need to grow regardless of circumstance.

The question is whether that food is healthy for them to consume. Happily, if you stick with the recommendations within, then you should be providing your children with a relatively healthy variety of nutrients, at least long enough for things to return to normal, and for their usual diet to resume. If in doubt, please consult your child's pediatrician or a knowledgeable nutritionist.

What About Those Food-Related Buzz Terms?

I'd imagine you've also heard various other food-related buzz terms like phytonutrients, antioxidants, and paleo, to name a few. Do any of them matter?

The short answer is, no, they do not.

I'm not saying foods with these attributes aren't healthy or beneficial, it's just that they're not certain to be necessary for survival. Beyond that, they're also most likely found in fresh foods which won't store in the pantry for months or years on end.

Of course, there are ways for you to store typically fresh foods besides in the refrigerator, specifically dehydrated and freeze-dried foods, to name two great examples. I tend to prefer freeze-dried foods for several reasons, including being more nutritious and longer-lasting than their dehydrated counterparts.

As such, if you really want to take your survival pantry to the next level, then please do consider adding freeze-dried foods to your pantry. The major problem, it seems, is that freeze-dried foods tend to be relatively expensive to purchase. Consequently, I wouldn't recommend them just yet; get the bulk of your pantry foods in order, as discussed in this book, and then move on to purchasing dehydrated or freeze-dried foods as money and time permit.

27 Grocery Store Foods to Stockpile

In this section, we're going to look at each category in reverse order to how they were introduced previously, mostly because that's the way I researched the topic. As such, we'll look at fiber, protein, fat, carbohydrates, calories, and end with vitamins and minerals. Remember, I've put it all together for you in the 57-point pantry foods to store checklist, if you need a handy reference.

Now, I don't want you to just skip directly to the checklist, even if you've downloaded it already. The reasoning is akin to just memorizing answers for a test: If you don't understand why and how to get to the answer for yourself, then you won't be able to make educated decisions beyond the list. For example, you could very well find other foods even better than those listed within, yet not realize it because you only focused on the answers to the test.

Regarding the Data Compiled Within

Before I get too far ahead of myself, I need to point out that the nutritional data cited throughout were taken directly from the United States Department of Agriculture, Agricultural Research Service in the event you want to check my numbers or research your own food choices.[6]

There are actually a few websites from which to get such data and I believe that they all show very similar numbers, but this one seemed as complete as I could have asked for and included all the important information we needed to compare, such as calories, protein, fiber and more. To get to the database I used, follow the link above and then click the website link that says, FNDDS Nutrient Values.xlsx or you can download the Excel file directly here, which comes directly from the USDA website.[7]

Understand that their data is calculated based on a 100-gram serving of food which, with regards to a portion of meat, for example, is roughly the same size as a deck of playing cards. If you peruse the data like I did, you'll notice that some numbers may seem too good to be true, such as high levels of fat found in many cooking oils. This, of course, is a ridiculous amount of cooking oil to consume at any one time and, so, the numbers aren't always useful as a one-to-one comparison. After all, it's not like you're going to eat a playing-card sized amount of Crisco, well, I'd hope not, anyway.

In addition, data included here was taken as is so it may not be perfectly clear in some instances what food the data refers to as there are several thousand entries. Regardless, I looked for the most common foods I could find, at least as much I could make sense of it. For simplicity's sake, the names of food I included here were copied exactly as they appeared in the dataset so that you can reference it later, if you like.

Of course, there are many brands of these common foods available which will, no doubt, vary in their levels of the nutrients we're interested in, so just because I list canned tuna as having roughly twenty-nine grams of protein, you may well find a brand that has more or less protein than that. Please check labels if you're particularly concerned about precise nutrient levels.

Realize, too, that some foods are fortified with a wide assortment of vitamins, fiber, protein, and other nutrients. It may be wise, therefore, to specifically look for foods that include such fortifications when grocery shopping to maximize your nutrition.

Last, I attempted to include only foods that are commonly found in grocery stores and, thus, you won't see any unusual foods in this list (not until we get to the superfoods list, anyway), or eccentric ethnic foods which may well contain more of a particular nutrient gram-for-gram.

Food Longevity is a Must

Understand that, although we need vitamins, minerals, calories, and macronutrients, we also need to ensure food longevity. After all, if the food can't last longer than a few days in your pantry, then what's the point in worrying about vitamin and mineral yields? There isn't one.

Clearly, the ability to store food for months or even years without refrigeration is what we want. Sadly, this quickly excludes the most nutrient-dense foods in their most nutritious state, specifically fresh fruits, vegetables, meat, and dairy, simply because they must be refrigerated or frozen to avoid spoilage.

Of course, it is certainly possible to keep these foods viable for several months or even longer by utilizing storage methods such as dehydrating, freeze-drying, and canning, as I briefly mentioned earlier; you should take advantage of these storage methods as much as possible after you're finished with my shelf-stable food recommendations.

In any case, this section of the book is about gathering common foods already found at your local grocery store with the intent of maximizing their usefulness to your survival during hard times. To satisfy this requirement, we're going to opt for canned and packaged foods. Basically, everything found in the middle of most grocery stores is fair game.

Let's get started.

Foods Highest in Fiber

Realize that disasters often bring additional stress and stress often induces digestive problems. As such, including plenty of fiber in your diet may be beneficial to keeping your bowels regular. On the other hand, it could just stop you up for days on end; only you know how your body might react.

Remember, too, that the average adult only needs between 21-38 grams of fiber per day. Fortunately, it's not like you need all your fiber intake from a single food source. Regardless, if food is scarce, then you may need to look to foods that provide significantly more of a dietary need than you otherwise would, including fiber intake.

Let's start by looking at the top ten items in the dataset, sorted by total dietary fiber:

Main food description	Fiber (g)
Cereal (General Mills Fiber One)	46.2
Wheat bran, unprocessed	42.8
Cereal (Kellogg's All-Bran Bran Buds)	42.5
Nutritional powder mix (Kellogg's Special K20 Protein Water)	37.5
Cocoa powder, not reconstituted	37
Cereal (Kellogg's All-Bran)	29.3
Flax seeds	27.3
Chia seeds	27.3
Yeast	26.9
Coffee substitute, dry powder	23.3

At the top of the list you'll find a cereal, specifically a fiber-fortified brand. You'll also find wheat bran, another cereal, a few different powders, and foods we'll discuss later, that being flax seeds and chia seeds. Finally, some sort of coffee substitute rounds out the top ten.

Notice, too, that the amount of fiber drops in half as we get to the bottom of the top ten. Even so, you'd still be getting nearly all the fiber your body requires from this single food source. Granted, you're not going to be consuming 100 grams of any of the bottom items from the top ten list, especially the seeds, yeast, or coffee substitute. At least, I sure hope not. Although there's a few items to consider within the top ten, let's look at the next ten on the list:

Main food description	Fiber (g)
Cereal or granola bar (General Mills Fiber One Chewy Bar)	22.5
Cereal or granola bar, high fiber, coated with non-chocolate yogurt coating	22.5
Cereal (Kashi Good Friends)	21.7
Cereal (Uncle Sam)	20.3
Cereal (Kashi GOLEAN)	20.1
Cereal (General Mills Fiber One Caramel Delight)	19.1
Cereal (General Mills Fiber One Honey Clusters)	19
Vegetable mixture, dried	19
Papad, grilled or broiled	18.6
Cereal (Barbara's Puffins)	18.5

Cereals stand out as holding eight of the next ten spots. I'd say that's telling us something, wouldn't you? At the very least, the difference in total fiber from the top to the bottom of the next ten on the list doesn't change much, which is encouraging.

I won't bore you by showing you list after list of foods that may not be useful. I will, on the other hand, include an assortment of notable selections as I further perused the next few hundred entries in the dataset:

Main food description	Fiber (g)
Nutritional powder mix, high protein (Slim Fast)	18.2
Sesame seeds	16.9
Cookie, oatmeal, reduced fat, NS as to raisins	16.1
Cake, chocolate, with icing, diet	14.9
Snack cake, chocolate, with icing or filling, reduced fat and calories	14.9
Popcorn, air-popped, unbuttered	14.4
Almonds, unroasted	12.5
Nutrition bar (Snickers Marathon Protein Bar)	12.5
Bread, wheat or cracked wheat, reduced calorie and/or high fiber, toasted	12.2
Sunflower seeds, plain, unsalted	11.1
Cookie, brownie, reduced fat, NS as to icing	11.1
Sunflower seeds, plain, salted	11
Crackers, gluten free, plain	10.2
Black, brown, or Bayo beans, canned, drained, fat not added in cooking	10.1
Oats, raw	10.1
Peanuts, roasted, salted	9.4
Granola, homemade	8.9

I tried to pick out a variety of foods that were potential candidates to include, usually opting for the first food that I came to. For instance, the first time I saw a bread appear, I simply grabbed the first one I encountered, which happened to be wheat or cracked wheat bread. The thing is that you may not be able—or even want—to purchase this specific type of bread. It's the general category of wheat bread, or merely bread, that you should focus on.

Because of this, I don't want you to believe that you must only get one very specific item because it's on a table of foods I include here. Rather, the idea is to use these tables to get an idea of what types of foods or general food groups may be best to include in your own list.

With that in mind, I did notice that breakfast cereals of all kinds continued to show up further down the dataset. As such, cereals will make the list of foods to include for sure.

Furthermore, as I continued to peruse the dataset, I ran into various seeds and nuts over again as well. Sesame seeds, almonds, sunflower seeds, and peanuts made the table above, though there were plenty of others I could have included, such as pistachios, pecans, and hazelnuts, to name a few. Nuts in some form or another will make the list as well.

There are, of course, sometimes alternatives which may be better options than the original food. Peanut butter, for instance, would be a great way to store peanuts; similarly, almond butter is likely a healthier alternative, though almond butter usually needs to be refrigerated after opening, whereas peanut butter often does not.

A few other items continued to show up repeatedly, including breads, popcorn, crackers and, to a lesser extent, cookies. Finally, assorted canned beans round out the bottom of the list, many of which—such as kidney beans, white beans, and pinto beans—I didn't bother to include in the table above.

Now, even though a food group showed up many times—and even made the table above—that doesn't mean we can or should attempt to include it in our pantry. For instance, even though breads showed up quite often, they're not a good shelf-stable food to rely upon. The problem being, of course, that breads don't store well for long periods of time. A most lasting solution would be to stockpile the ingredients necessary to make your own bread, particularly wheat to make flour, as well as salt, sugar, oil, and yeast. Granted, most folks probably wouldn't want to go to such trouble, especially for short-term disaster scenarios, so you'll have to decide whether doing so will work for your situation.

Popcorn is another food group which doesn't store well. In this case, you could purchase popcorn kernels—the kind you fry in a pan—along with some oil and now you have both a shelf-stable alternative to already made popcorn and a tasty treat.

Crackers and cookies are shelf-stable, albeit some more than others. To increase longevity, you could further package these types of snack foods in FoodSaver bags or even freeze them. Furthermore, you might choose crackers which have less oil content to avoid them going rancid faster. Moreover, cookies, like bread, could be made from scratch with minimal ingredients, if that interests you.

Finally, while I didn't include such foods in the table above because they weren't very significant fiber sources, a few other common grocery store foods did show up on the list eventually, including potato chips, pancake mix, pretzels, and pastas, all of which tend to be in most folks everyday pantries.

Foods Highest in Protein

Remember how we said that protein was the building block of life? That's makes them important and, in fact, the body needs protein to repair and maintain cells and produce energy, among other things. Be sure you're getting enough, and bear in mind that the average adult male needs about one and a half times that of a female to be healthy.

Although protein is found in many sources, by and large, it's mostly found in meats, dairy, and nuts. Oddly, though, traditional meats barely break into the top ten via pork skin rinds, though I'm not sure that even counts as a meat source, as shown here:

Main food description	Protein (g)
Nutritional powder mix, whey based, NFS	78.13
Nutritional powder mix, protein, NFS	78.13
Tuna, fresh, dried	76.25
Nutritional powder mix (EAS Whey Protein Powder)	66.67
Salmon, dried	64.06
Fish, NS as to type, dried	62.82
Cod, dried, salted	62.82
Pork skin rinds	61.3
Squid, dried	58.94
Nutritional powder mix (Isopure)	58.14

Interestingly, there are two standouts within the top ten list alone that I would strongly encourage you to include, specifically whey protein powder (discussed in the superfoods section) and dried tuna. Most everything else on the list is either some sort of dried fish that you may not be able to acquire, or another protein powder.

Unfortunately, the top ten list of highest in protein foods isn't very helpful. What about the next ten on the list? Let's find out:

Main food description	Protein (g)
Octopus, dried	56.52
Herring, dried, salted	55.71
Nutritional powder mix, protein, soy based, NFS	55.56
Nutritional powder mix, high protein (Herbalife)	53.57
Nutritional powder mix, high protein, NFS	53.57
Shrimp, dried	51.7
Soybean meal	51.46
Textured vegetable protein, dry	51.46
Nutritional powder mix, light (Muscle Milk)	50
Nutritional powder mix, protein, light, NFS	50

Here, again, we see that half the list contains various powder mixes, and the rest is some sort of fish or sea creature, most of which aren't going to be found at your local grocery store, at least, not in a shelf-stable form.

After perusing the massive protein dataset, it became clear to me that meats of all kinds, such as turkey, pork, chicken, beef—and even oddball choices like bear, opossum, and ostrich—show up repeatedly further down in the data, dominating the next few hundred contenders.

In any case, meats are usually listed as being cooked, baked, or fried, none of which, I assume, is quite the same as canned. Assorted fish options showed up often as well, including ones you might suspect, such as tuna fish or salmon, but even uncommon choices like octopus or squid. Anyhow, I would suggest that if you can get any type of canned meat or fish that you'll consume from your local grocery store, then go for it. As such, canned meats and canned fish make the list for sure.

Arby's "We have the meats" slogan feels rather appropriate here, doesn't it? But what if we don't have the meats, what then? We must look elsewhere, specifically to alternative protein sources, such as dairy and legumes. Unfortunately, this list gets even shorter because most every dairy item we could include needs to be kept refrigerated, specifically, milk and cheese, though there are a few powdered dairy options available if you're willing to seek them out. It seems we're almost stuck with beans, though not all is lost, since moving on down the list does produce some possible choices:

Main food description	Protein (g)
Cheese, Parmesan, dry grated, fat free	40
Milk, dry, not reconstituted, NS as to fat content	35.1
Pumpkin seeds, NFS	29.84
Tuna, canned, oil pack	29.13
Wheat germ, plain	29.1
Peanuts, roasted, salted	28.03
Peanut butter, reduced fat	25.9
Chicken, canned, meat only	25.3
Turkey, canned	25.3

Main food description (cont.)	Protein (g)
Sardines, canned in oil	24.62
Almonds, unroasted	21.15
Almond butter	20.96
Sunflower seeds, plain, unsalted	19.33
Cereal (Kellogg's Special K)	17.79
Bread, wheat or cracked wheat, reduced calorie and/or high fiber, toasted	14.64
White beans, canned, drained, fat not added in cooking	10.84
Cookie, peanut butter, sugar free	10.34
Black, brown, or Bayo beans, canned, drained, fat not added in cooking	8.87
Potato chips, reduced fat, unsalted	7.1

Does this look familiar to you, because it sure does to me? I'm seeing nuts, beans, a cereal, as well as cookies and potato chips. Besides the addition of a few canned meats and dairy products, this table looks an awful lot like the fiber table. Granted, I'm the one that hand-picked these foods but, trust me, there weren't any better everyday shelf-stable foods to include.

So, where are we now?

Besides canned meats and fish, you could choose to include any sort of powdered dairy product—such as dry milk powder—which not only adds protein in a shelf-stable form but also makes cereal enjoyable. That said, powdered milk doesn't have quite the same texture as normal store-bought milk. Regardless, I'd say powdered milk will suffice for cereal when that's all you have to rely upon.

Beyond that we're again looking at nuts, seeds, and beans as discussed in the fiber section, so I won't rehash them here except to say that most canned beans contain somewhere between 5-9 grams of protein per 100-gram serving whereas canned meats vary significantly, yet tend to have plenty more protein per serving. Anyway, just so that you have something to go by, at roughly 400 grams per average can of beans (15.25-ounce cans assumed) a single can of beans could get you close to your protein needs each day if you had no other option.

The grams of protein really drop off near the end of the table above, particularly when we look at including snacks foods, such as cookies and potato chips. Honestly, I wouldn't bother with including these foods for your protein needs and it's not a great way to round out the list either. Fortunately, we do have plenty of canned meat choices (really, almost any canned meats will suffice), canned beans (again, plenty of choices here), dry milk and cheese powders, some nuts, and a few possible snacks. I say we can work with this.

Remember that adults need somewhere between 40-70 grams of protein each day. That's not a lot of protein if we could include fresh meats each day, which is certainly difficult to do without refrigeration. Canning or smoking meats at home would help, but those topics are outside of the scope of this book. If you're interested in such methods, then please do peruse Amazon for a book or watch YouTube videos, as there are many resources out there to show you how.

Foods Highest in Fat

When you think about fatty foods, what comes to mind? Perhaps ice cream, cookies, and chocolate, to name a few. Luckily, since the average adult only needs about 20-35 grams of fat per day, we don't need to stock the most fattening foods. Regardless, it can't hurt to know which foods are more fattening than not. With that in mind, let's look at the top ten:

Main food description	Total Fat (g)
Lard	100
Shortening, animal	100
Vegetable oil, NFS	100
Almond oil	100
Corn oil	100
Cottonseed oil	100
Olive oil	100
Peanut oil	100
Rapeseed oil	100
Canola and soybean oil	100

Besides lard and animal shortening, as you can clearly see, cooking oils top the list. In fact, when I looked at the next ten on the list (which I won't bother to show you this time) I noticed that cooking oils absolutely dominate. It's not until we get beyond the top twenty that we encounter something besides an oil, mostly assorted butters.

In any case, because oils are both useful for cooking some meals and contain the most fat content possible—which your body does require—you should absolutely include them in your pantry. Personally, I would stick with healthier oils, such as extra virgin olive oil, but the choice is yours.

Besides cooking oils, here's a sampling of other fat-rich possibilities to consider, which I'm going to split into two lists to make discussing them easier:

Main food description	Total Fat (g)
Shortening, vegetable	99.97
Butter, stick, salted	81.11
Mayonnaise, regular	74.85
Pecans, unsalted	72.81
Salad dressing, NFS, for sandwiches	64.2
Mixed nuts, without peanuts, unsalted	55.54
Almond butter	55.5
Peanut butter, lower sugar	54.89
Peanuts, roasted, salted	52.5
Topping, chocolate, hard coating	44.1
Flax seeds	42.16
Chia seeds	42.16

Here we're beginning to see a larger variety of foods for a change. Shortening, such as Crisco, and butter make the top of the list—both of which can be considered shelf-stable—followed closely by mayonnaise and even salad dressings, both of which surprised me.

We also find that nuts make the list again in various forms, as well as those that I didn't include in the above table to save space, such as pecans and hazelnuts. Most nuts are going to be high in fat content, so they can be added to the list of foods you should include for this purpose too.

We also find that flax seeds and chia seeds make the list here as well, but they'll be discussed later in the superfoods section, so, for now, we're going to leave those two alone. Let's move on to the remaining group of possibilities:

Main food description	Total Fat (g)
Potato chips, lightly salted	35.32
Cookie, with peanut butter filling, chocolate-coated	35.3
Milk chocolate candy, with almonds	34.4
TWIX Chocolate Fudge Cookie Bars	33.3
Cereal or granola bar with nuts, chocolate coated	31.2
Cookie, sugar or plain, sugar free	31.03
M&M's Peanut Butter Chocolate Candies	29.32

Main food description (cont.)	Total Fat (g)
Coffee, instant, pre-lightened and pre-sweetened with low calorie sweetener, not reconstituted	29.1
Trail mix with nuts and fruit	26.8
Milk, dry, not reconstituted, whole	26.71
Cake or cupcake, carrot, with icing or filling	26.5
Crackers, butter (Ritz)	26.43

Here again, we have an assortment of foods, especially snack foods like potato chips, chocolate bars, cake, and crackers. There's a cereal in the table also, and even instant coffee for those who cannot live without their morning coffee fix.

Really, chocolate and related candies showed up repeatedly, as well as various crackers, though Ritz crackers are about the only store-bought name brand that I recognized. And, although they were a bit too far down on the list to be included, graham crackers did show up, eventually; I'm sure most young children would happily eat them as a snack food regardless of their nutrient value.

To wrap up, I'd say it's clear that cooking oils along animal fats or shortening are a requirement to add to your pantry, and if you can include some form of butter, that would be great. Likewise, any sort of chocolates or nuts are fine choices as well.

Last, condiments such as mayonnaise and salad dressings could be useful additions in some cases. Although they would need to be refrigerated after opening, so I'm not sure I would bother with including them unless you have some form of off-grid refrigeration for when the power is out. I'd also suggest that if you simply cannot live without coffee, then include that too.

Foods Highest in Carbohydrates

Like I said earlier, carbohydrates are relatively easy to acquire since the average adult needs about 130 grams per day, but if you want to maximize carbs in your pantry foods, then look to breakfast cereals, snack foods, and sweets...oh, wait, I'm getting ahead of myself.

Let's look at the top ten now:

Main food description	Carbs (g)
Sugar substitute, stevia, powder	100
Sugar substitute, monk fruit, powder	100
Sugar, NFS	99.98
Sugar, white, granulated or lump	99.98
Sugar, white, confectioner's, powdered	99.77
Sugar substitute and sugar blend	99.72
Strawberry beverage powder, dry mix, not reconstituted	99.1
Fruit flavored drink, with high vitamin C, powdered, not reconstituted	98.94
Gumdrops	98.9
Sugar, cinnamon	98.63

As might be expected, actual sugar converts almost 100% to simple sugars. While granulated or powdered sugars are obviously needed for baking, they may not be so handy as a part of your survival pantry. In the above list, though, I did notice the fruit flavored drink mix and gumdrops as being two possibilities to consider.

Let's move on to the next ten in the dataset:

Main food description	Carbs (g)
Dietetic or low calorie candy, NFS	98.6
Dietetic or low calorie hard candy	98.6
Dietetic or low calorie mints	98.6
Tea, iced, instant, black, pre-sweetened, dry	98.55
Sugar, brown	98.09
Sugar, carmelized	98.09
Candy, NFS	98
Hard candy	98
Fruit flavored drink, powdered, not reconstituted	97.9
Sports drink, dry concentrate, not reconstituted	97.9

The first items I noticed were the few candies that made the table and, although they're not very specific, I can guess that most hard candy is pretty much the same when it comes to carbohydrate percentages. Besides that, the instant iced tea and sports drink are intriguing.

Here's what else I could find that may be of use to us:

Main food description	Carbs (g)
Coffee, instant, pre-sweetened with sugar, not reconstituted	95.22
Licorice	93.55
Skittles	90.78
Cereal (Kellogg's Corn Pops)	89.7
Fruit syrup	85.13
Hot chocolate / Cocoa, dry mix, not reconstituted	83.73
Honey	82.4
Crackers, saltine, reduced fat	82.3
Pretzels, hard, plain, salted	80.39
Tortilla chips, reduced fat, plain	79.07
Graham crackers	77.66
Cookie, gingersnaps	76.9
Cookie, shortbread, reduced fat	75.99
Potato chips, baked, plain	71.4
Jelly, all flavors	69.95

The first point I'd like to make is that, although I only included one type in the above table, cereals dominated the top few hundred results, like how meats dominated the protein category. My guess is because most cereals are made from grains, and grains tend to convert directly into simple sugars. Thus, cereals make the list of foods to include again, hands down.

Similarly, many other foods made mostly from grains tended toward the top of the dataset as well, such as chips, cookies, pretzels, and crackers. Thus, I'd say that any shelf-stable snacks are likely good candidates to include in your pantry and will offer a tasty load of carbohydrates.

Some condiments made the list too, including fruit syrup, honey, and jellies. Besides that, instant coffee made the list as well as two unexpected additions, licorice and skittles.

Many foods further down the list ran the gamut of snack foods and condiments and were far too numerous to mention here.

Foods Highest in Calories

Unlike the other categories, calories are one where I would almost assuredly want more of it in my foods during a survival situation than not. And since the average adult needs between 1600-3000 calories (more active folks and males need more) it behooves us to look for shelf-stable foods which are highest in calories, so let's look at the top ten now:

Main food description	Energy (kcal)
Lard	902
Shortening, animal	902
Corn oil	900
Industrial oil as ingredient in food	892
Coconut oil	892
Vegetable oil, NFS	886
Almond oil	884
Cottonseed oil	884
Olive oil	884
Peanut oil	884

This table looks eerily like the dietary fats table did, in that animal fats and oils dominate the top ten without question. The next ten in the dataset are all cooking oils too, and it's not until we get to number twenty-seven in the dataset, salt pork, that we see something besides a cooking oil or fat. Various forms of butter take over for a while and then we finally get to the following:

Main food description	Energy (kcal)
Pecans, unsalted	697
Mayonnaise, regular	680
Peanut butter, lower sodium and lower sugar	624
Sunflower seeds, plain, unsalted	582
Cookie, with peanut butter filling, chocolate-coated	562
Cheese flavored corn snacks (Cheetos)	560
Potato chips, lightly salted	559
Chocolate, sweet or dark, with almonds	553
Caesar dressing	542
Flax seeds	534
Chia seeds	534
Beef jerky	410
Cake, chocolate, with icing, diet	409
Hot chocolate / Cocoa, dry mix, not reconstituted	398

Nuts and seeds also dominate for a while in all their varieties. Mayonnaise makes a brief appearance again, and then we get to the typical snack foods, including cookies, chips, chocolate, and cake. Again, we see flax seeds and chia seeds make the list, cocoa mix, and one new entry, beef jerky.

Foods Highest in Vitamins and Minerals

We're going to look at vitamins and minerals a bit differently than the other categories. Why? Because it's a giant mess to compile data for literally dozens of different vitamins and minerals, especially when the legwork has already been done, as you'll soon see. Besides, your eyes would glaze over, and my head might implode if I tried to sort through it all.

With that in mind, most of us know that the foods highest in vitamins and minerals are the fresh fruits, vegetables, meats, and dairy, which are difficult to store without refrigeration.

Lucky for us, many of the foods I've already suggested previously include a variety of vitamins and minerals to some extent, so it's not like we're going to be completely deficient if that's all we had to rely upon.

In any case, we still want to maximize our nutritional intake as much as possible. So, besides the foods already mentioned above, what foods can we add to supplement our vitamin intake? The major vitamins are as follows:[8]

- **Vitamin A**: Sweet potatoes, carrots, spinach, fortified cereals;

- **Vitamin C**: Red and green peppers, kiwis, oranges and other citrus fruits, strawberries, broccoli, tomatoes;
- **Vitamin D**: Fish liver oils, fatty fish, fortified milk products, fortified cereals;
- **Vitamin E**: Fortified cereals, sunflower seeds, almonds, peanut butter, vegetable oils;
- **Vitamin K**: Green vegetables like spinach, collards, and broccoli; Brussels sprouts; cabbage;
- **Choline**: Milk, liver, eggs, peanuts.

The B-vitamins are found in a variety of foods as well. Here's a brief list:[9]

- **B1**: Pork, berries, legumes, lean meats, nuts, soy milk;
- **B2**: Eggs, dark green vegetables, fish, grains, lean meat, mushrooms;
- **B3**: Sunflower seeds, tuna, poultry, potato, cottage cheese, liver;
- **B5**: Organ meats, avocados, broccoli, mushrooms;
- **B6**: Green beans, whole grains, spinach, fish, bananas;
- **B7**: Soy products, egg yolks, fish, organ meats, cheese, sweet potatoes;
- **B9**: Green leafy vegetables, citrus juice, legumes, tofu, tomato juice;

- **B12**: Milk, fish, fortified breakfast cereal, eggs, shellfish.

With regards to minerals, the list is also rather large:[10]

- **Calcium**: Milk, yogurt, hard cheeses, fortified cereals, kale;
- **Chloride**: Found in table salt (as sodium chloride);
- **Chromium**: Broccoli, potatoes, meats, poultry, fish, some cereals;
- **Copper**: Seafood, nuts, seeds, wheat bran cereals, whole grains;
- **Fluoride**: Fluoridated water, some sea fish;
- **Iodine**: Seafood, dairy products, processed foods, iodized salt;
- **Iron**: Fortified cereals, beans, lentils, beef, turkey, soy beans, spinach;
- **Magnesium**: Green leafy vegetables, nuts, dairy, soybeans, potatoes, whole wheat, quinoa;
- **Manganese**: Nuts, beans and other legumes, tea, whole grains;
- **Molybdenum**: Legumes, leafy vegetables, grains, nuts;
- **Phosphorus**: Milk, dairy, peas, meat, eggs, some cereals and breads;
- **Potassium**: Potatoes, bananas, yogurt, milk, yellowfin tuna, soybeans, and a variety of fruits and vegetables;

- **Selenium**: Organ meats, seafood, dairy, Brazil nuts;
- **Sodium**: Foods made with added salt, such as processed foods;
- **Zinc**: Red meats, some seafood, fortified cereals.

Here, again, I see cereals pop up repeatedly, as well as an assortment of nuts and seeds, legumes, and dairy products. Since we've already covered these food groups, let's briefly talk about the most important foods with regards to vitamins and minerals that I didn't cover yet, fruits and vegetables.

For your survival pantry to work like you need it to, you'll need to include a variety of canned vegetables and fruits as well. Everything is fair game, from canned corn and green beans to diced tomatoes and tomato sauce. Really, any form of vegetable that you're willing to eat is great to add. Try to focus on foods which are canned and not jarred because of the expectation that you will consume all the canned vegetables in one meal.

The same goes for canned fruits, from sliced pears and peaches to mandarin oranges and fruit cocktails; opt for canned fruit packed in its own juices if you prefer less sugar for some reason. Fruit in small snack-sized cups would be good to store as well, particularly if you have younger children. Jellies too, would be useful to include and likely won't go bad even if unrefrigerated for weeks or months due to their high sugar content.

Please don't ignore such an important component to your survival pantry! It's these foods that will keep your vitamin and mineral levels at appropriate levels and make meals even tastier.

A Handful More Additions to Consider

While stockpiling the aforementioned canned foods is a great start, I would also encourage you add the following items to your survival pantry for reasons that I'll explain:

- Canned soups, chilis, chowders (e.g., vegetable beef, beef stew, chicken noodle, chicken with rice, tomato soup, chunky chicken soup, chili with beans, clam chowder, etc.) since they tend to combine a variety of nutritious foods into one can and only need heated up to be eaten.
- Any powdered drink mixes or canned drinks (e.g., lemonade drink mix, fruit punch mix, hot chocolate mix, V8 juice, etc.) most of which are fortified with vitamin C and offer a tasty alternative to water alone. I would avoid sodas, unless you already consume them regularly.

- Pasta sauce (e.g., tomato based or Alfredo) because they'll be expected when we discuss spaghetti and macaroni in the bulk foods section.

Shelf-Stable Foods Recap

So, what did we end up with from the grocery store? For starters, I see some tasty breakfast foods, mostly in the form of cereals, though we'll discuss additional choices in the next section. Stockpile a variety of different cereals and you'll be set for your first meal of the day, although we will discuss other options in the bulk foods section. In any case, be sure to add powdered milk (also discussed in the bulk foods section) to your food storage, so the cereal is appetizing.

There were also plenty of snack foods, such as potato chips, cookies, pretzels, crackers, popcorn, chocolate, and hard candies. Granted, these foods won't provide loads of nutrients in a single serving, and they won't last nearly as long in the pantry as most other foods we will discuss, but they will be a welcome change for your taste buds, especially for families with children who usually expect a variety of snack foods throughout the day.

Drinks are covered too. We've included powdered drink mixes, lemonade, hot chocolate mix, instant coffee, iced tea, and V8 juice. Unless your family is accustomed to only drinking water throughout the day, I would ensure you have a variety of drink alternatives to choose from.

What about actual meals? That's a bit more difficult until we cover bulk foods. Nevertheless, we've added the basics for a wide range of meals, such as canned beans, meats, fish, vegetables and of course, a wide variety of canned soups, chilis, and chowders, each of which are meals in and of themselves.

There are some condiments included, such as mayonnaise, jelly, honey (discussed more in the superfoods section), peanut butter and, of course, plenty of nuts and seeds. It's up to you whether you include these types of foods, especially oddball items like mayonnaise that may not be of use. Other foods, especially honey, peanut butter, and even jelly, could all prove useful, particularly if you're willing to make bread for sandwiches.

I would include a variety of seasonings, particularly salt and pepper, yet it couldn't hurt to ensure your pantry is stocked full of a wide range of seasonings. Understand, too, that appetite fatigue—characterized by a lack of interest in food—is a real concern with bland or repetitive foods and that seasonings will go a long way to minimizing appetite fatigue due to meals made from the same basic and repeated food.

I should reiterate that many of these foods can be made to last even longer if sealed in FoodSaver bags, particularly snack foods like crackers and pretzels. That said, other foods such as nuts may not last very long no matter what you do, due to higher fat or oil content which tends to cause them to go rancid regardless.

11 Bulk Foods to Stockpile

Eventually, you're going to find that stockpiling canned and boxed foods at your local grocery store isn't the only food you should store. You're going to find that you want even more food storage and that you want it fast, cheap, and inexpensive.

There's only one way to do that I'm aware of and that's by purchasing food in bulk. The thing is that even buying basic foods in bulk can cost more than one would prefer. Worse, most bulk foods sold to the public come in large bags—often 25-50 pounds— which are heavy and then you must do something with that food to keep it viable for years, to keep rodents and bugs out, and just to make it easier on you to utilize.

There is a faster, easier solution and it's called The Church of Jesus Christ of Latter-day Saints Home Storage Center, or the LDS Cannery for short. Here, you can purchase a variety of bulk foods, all of which have been properly sealed in #10 cans with oxygen absorbers, though you may find some foods like dry milk powder packaged in Mylar pouches instead.

Why go to all the trouble of buying bulk foods that are more expensive pound for pound and then repack it in Mylar bags and/or buckets yourself which you'll also have to purchase, when you can get everything you want already properly sealed and packaged for you?

Unless you have some very specific health-related reason, such as not being able to eat wheat, for example, then the LDS Home Storage Center is without a doubt the best place to buy bulk foods that most of us eat on a regular basis.

What You Should Know

Personally, I've purchased bulk foods from their Home Storage Centers several times over the past decade and I've never been disappointed. That said, there are a few things you should be aware of, so let's discuss them now.

Must I Be a Member of The Church?

Usually, the first question most people have when I suggest they buy bulk foods from the LDS Home Storage Center is Do I have to be a member of the church?

Luckily, the answer is no; you don't. I'm not personally a member, but I do have various family and friends who are. Regardless, the church doesn't require you to be a member to buy bulk foods from their Home Storage Centers.

While I have occasionally heard of unconfirmed stories where people who are not members of the church were not allowed to purchase food for whatever reason, I've never personally been told this by anyone I know. To the best of my knowledge, they're happy to sell you food even if you're not a member.

To be clear, you shouldn't pretend to be a member of the church. Be honest and tell them "I'm not a member but I would like to purchase food from you," and I'd be willing to bet they're fine with that. If whomever you talk to gives you the runaround, then take it up with the local church leadership and get a clarification. Contact the local Stake Center and I'm sure they can help you out; you can use this locator map to help find the proper contact information if necessary.[11]

The only restriction I'm aware of is that some Home Storage Centers may limit the amount of bulk foods non-members can purchase at any one time. I'm told members have no such limit, so don't go in expecting that you can purchase thousands of dollars' worth of food on your first visit. Of course, be sure to verify what's allowed before making any assumptions.

They'll probably also want you to pay by check. At least, that's what I've always experienced when I went. In fact, they may not even accept cash or credit cards, though some centers may accept other forms of payment besides a check these days; be sure to ask what forms of payment your local Home Storage Center accepts.

Is There a Home Storage Center Near Me?

Usually, the second thing most people ask is whether there's a Home Storage Center near them or if they must drive to Utah. Ok, maybe that's not the second question, but it's always good to know if you have a long way to drive or not. Here's an incomplete map of Storage Centers from their website, with over 100 locations across the U.S. and Canada:

As you can see, there are many Home Storage Centers spread out across the country and, like I said, the above map is incomplete. Your best bet is to peruse their list of locations to find the center closest to you.[12]

Must I Can My Own Food?

It used to be that you when you went to the LDS Cannery that you'd have to work for it and literally spend a few hours canning food! In fact, it was customary, at least when I used to go, that everybody there would work to can each other's food until it was all done.

That is, if there were sixty cans of spaghetti ordered because multiple groups would be there at the same time, but you only ordered twenty cans yourself, well, you would be helping to can all the spaghetti whether you wanted to or not; the same was true for all the other foods there. Yes, it was work, but I never minded because I received good food at a great price, and I was able to help others do the same. It was a win-win, in my opinion.

As awesome as all that sounds, the process has become even easier because nearly all Home Storage Centers have gone away from canning foods on their premises and simply stockpile bulk foods that have already been properly sealed in #10 cans. This is great news because it means that you and I must no longer work to can our bulk foods. We simply show up with an order form and check in hand.

Questions to Ask Them by Phone

The first thing you're going to want to do is to visit their Home Storage Locations Center page and find the center nearest you. Hopefully there's one relatively nearby and, even if there is one close, I wouldn't just show up unannounced. Call them first and ask:[13]

1. **I'm not a member of the church. Can I still purchase food from you?** If they say no, talk to the local stake leadership referenced previously to verify this.
2. **What method of payment do you accept?** Most likely, payment is by check only.
3. **Do I need to make an appointment?** Usually, they like to know who's coming and when.

4. **Is there a limit to how much I can purchase at one time?** If so, is that limit a dollar amount, the number of cans/cases, by weight, or what? Remember, too, that you'll need to be able to transport home whatever you buy, so be sure you have both the space in your vehicle and that it can handle the weight.
5. **When are you open for business?** Most storage centers have very limited hours because the people who run them are volunteers; regardless, you can get an idea of their hours of operation from the same webpage referenced previously.[14]

It probably couldn't hurt to also verify that their Home Storage Center has their food already canned too, or if you still must do it yourself for some unexpected reason. They may also have some foods available for purchase in bulk bags which have not been canned, if interested.

Ask them if there is anything else you should know before coming, such as directions, because the building is hard to find or perhaps where to park.

Finally, I should point out that the church has a program where they open their Home Storage Centers to families—usually church members, though not always—who need assistance because they can't afford to purchase foods and other common household goods due to financial hardship or for whatever reason. They call this program the *Bishop's Storehouse*.

I mention this not to suggest that you should go begging for food but, rather, because their Home Storage Centers often double as the Bishop's Storehouse, which means that the volunteers there may want to know if you're there to request help from the Bishop's Storehouse or if you're there to purchase food instead.

Moreover, sometimes their Home Storage Centers are only open on one day for traditional purchases and then another day as the Bishop's Storehouse. For instance, your local Home Storage Center may be open on Wednesdays and Saturdays, but they only allow purchases on Wednesday and reserve Saturday to act as the Bishop's Storehouse, which means Saturday would be off limits to you. I'm not saying that's how they all work whatsoever. Just be sure to clarify when you're allowed to show up if they didn't do that already.

What Foods Can I Actually Buy?

You can purchase many bulk foods through their Home Storage Centers, including dry beans (black, pinto, refried), wheat (red and white), oats, pasta (spaghetti and macaroni), potato flakes, white rice, and sugar. You can also buy tastier and sometimes more nutritious foods, like carrots, apple slices, milk powder, cocoa mix, and more. Review their current list of foods via the order form links to get the complete list and current pricing.[15]

Usually, their list of available foods doesn't change much, if at all, over the years. They do, of course, occasionally update their prices once or twice a year, so be sure to check back using the links provided previously.

What if I Don't Want to Visit a Cannery?

I'm not sure why you wouldn't want to visit a nearby Home Storage Center unless it's just too far away or you can't physically move the cans around on your own, but if that's the case and you still want to purchase foods through the LDS Church then you may do so through their website.[16]

You are going to pay more for the same foods you'd find in their Home Storage Centers, but it's still often cheaper than other online sites. Obviously, you'll still have to pay appropriate shipping rates and fees and, no, you don't have to be a Church member for this option either, but you will have to register an online account.

How Do Prices Compare?

This is usually the biggest question to consider. Honestly, the best way to find out is to start searching for cheaper options. Go online and search for the term *buy bulk foods online* and you'll find several viable options, including bulkfoods.com, costco.com, allbulkfoods.com, and beprepared.com, among others.[17,18,19,20]

I've shopped a few places in the past and tend to prefer beprepared.com, but even they sometimes can't compete with the prices the LDS Home Storage Centers offer online, let alone in the Home Storage Centers. Let's look at a few examples below just to get an idea.

The following prices are as of the time of this writing during the spring of 2019; prices are subject to change.

If I buy 50 lbs. of hard red wheat, I would pay:

- $92.98 at bulkfoods.com (for two organic 25 lb. bags)
- $32.79 at allbulkfoods.com (for one 50 lb. bag)
- $54.95 at beprepared.com (for one 38 lb. super pail)
- $31.50 at local LDS Center (for nine #10 cans at 5.5 lbs. each) OR $20 for two 25 lb. bags

If I buy 50 lbs. of black beans:

- $86.98 at bulkfoods.com (for two 25 lb. bags of black turtle beans)
- $61.65 at allbulkfoods.com (for one 50 lb. bag of black turtle beans)
- $79.95 at beprepared.com (for one 41 lb. super pail)
- $49.50 at LDS Center (for nine #10 cans at 5.5 lbs. each)

If I buy 50 lbs. of white rice:

- $119.90 at bulkfoods.com (for two organic 25 lb. bags)
- $38.10 at allbulkfoods.com (for one 50 lb. bag of long grain white rice)
- $69.95 at beprepared.com (for one 40 lb. super pail)
- $45.00 at LDS Center (for nine #10 cans at 5.4 lbs. each)

If I buy 40 lbs. of spaghetti noodles:

- $70.38 bulkfoods.com (for two 20 lb. bags)
- $45.14 at allbulkfoods.com (for two 20 lb. bags)
- $167.40 at beprepared.com (for twelve #10 cans at about 3.2 lbs. each)

- $67.50 at LDS Center (for fifteen #10 cans at 2.7 lbs. each)

If I buy 50 lbs. of regular rolled oats:

- $71.95 at bulkfoods.com (for one 50 lb. bag)
- $30.87 at allbulkfoods.com (for one 50 lb. bag)
- $69.98 at beprepared.com (for two 24 lb. super pail buckets)
- $72.00 at LDS Center (for eighteen #10 cans at 2.8 lbs. each)

Price Comparison Takeaways

The first thing you may notice is that prices vary widely, even when only comparing a handful of foods. That's to be somewhat expected since companies offer a wide variety of choices, but I honestly wasn't expecting it to be this dramatic of a difference. There's a reason for this, as I'll explain in a minute.

And, although I tried to price compare similar items, sometimes it just wasn't possible. Even comparing something as simple as wheat was difficult since, for instance, the bulkfoods.com price was for organic red wheat, which, I suspect, increases the price drastically.

I should point out that the allbulkfoods.com prices seem reasonable at first but remember that you'll have to pay for shipping charges which can get rather expensive. To give you an idea of just how much it can be, I decided to estimate shipping charges after adding only the rolled oats to my cart and they wanted over $53 to ship to me in Washington state via UPS ground.

Bulkfoods.com, on the other hand, offers heavily discounted shipping rates on order over $75 to the lower 48 states; the website stated it would be a $5 shipping charge, yet for some reason they wanted to charge me $12 to ship my order; my guess was because I didn't yet qualify for the over $75 order requirement. Not taking advantage of their shipping offer increased shipping fees to more than the allkbulkfoods.com charge! The last choice, beprepared.com, wanted to charge a flat rate of $9.

Finally, out of curiosity, I checked the LDS online shipping rate for 18 cans of the rolled oats at an online total of $79.50 and they wanted a flat $3 shipping fee. That's much more reasonable.

Clearly, when taking shipping rates into consideration, the cheapest price isn't always the best choice. Like I said previously, I've been happy with purchases from beprepared.com in the past, and if you must choose an online company to buy bulk foods from, I would recommend them. The LDS online store is reasonably priced as well and apparently has even better shipping rates than anyone else I checked on, though I've never purchased directly from their website.

Remember, too, that you may have to repackage the bulk foods for long-term storage which can get a bit expensive even when doing it all yourself with Mylar bags, oxygen absorbers, and relatively cheap plastic buckets. On a positive note, the beprepared.com price is for bulk foods which are properly stored, and you'll even end up with a quality bucket you can make use of afterwards as a bonus. The LDS cans are also properly stored, but in #10 cans, which may prove slightly less useful than a large bucket during a disaster scenario.

While I can imagine that you might find one or two examples of online bulk foods which are, after all things are considered, less expensive than a local LDS Home Storage Center but you surely can't beat their prices, particularly when you add in the cost of having to pay for shipping as well as the materials to repackage it yourself.

To be clear, what is included on the Home Storage Center Order Form is literally all they have to offer for sale.[21] Many online websites, on the other hand, offer a huge variety of bulk foods, including many foods the Church doesn't stock, organic options, non-GMO, and more. If you're looking for something specific either because of preference or dietary needs, you'll surely find what you're looking for online, though you may pay a hefty price for the privilege.

What Foods to Focus on Buying?

Remember that the main purpose of bulk foods is to provide your body with calories and not necessarily nutrients. I'm not saying you don't get any nutrients—you do get some vitamins and minerals from traditional bulk foods—but their main objective is to provide calories.

With that in mind, your main goal is to focus on buying bulk foods that are considered meal fillers or they're the food upon which a meal is often centered around. Specifically, I'm talking about the very basics like rice, beans, and noodles. Since these foods are inexpensive and usually remain viable for many decades, I'd encourage you to stockpile quite a bit.

How Much Are We Talking About?

This depends on a variety of factors, such as for how long you want to prepare for as well as how many adults are expected to be fed. Note: I simply treat children as adults for food storage purposes. You're welcome to use the LDS online calculator to get a quick idea of how much you might need to store, though there are other online calculator options.[22] Using the LDS version, in this case, to feed one adult for one year you would need to purchase:

- 400 lbs. of grain (wheat, rice, oats, barley, pasta, etc.)

- 60 lbs. of legumes (dried beans, split peas, lentils, nuts, etc.)
- 30 lbs. dairy products (powdered milk, cheese powder, canned cheese, etc.)
- 60 lbs. of sugar (white sugar, brown sugar, syrup, molasses, honey, etc.)
- 6 lbs. of leavening agents (yeast, baking powder, powdered eggs, etc.)
- 6 lbs. of salt (table salt, sea salt, soy sauce, bouillon, etc.)
- 30 lbs. of fats (vegetable oils, shortening, canned butter, etc.)
- 28 gallons of water (for a two-week supply)

Clearly, the above list looks like a lot to buy, and it is. If you were to stockpile enough grains to feed a family of four for a single year, for example, that would be 1,600 pounds of grains alone! And that's to say nothing of the other items on the list. Fortunately, we're not trying to get you by for quite that long and we're not relying on bulk foods alone, so don't panic yet.

A few things you might notice from the list above are that not all the items suggested can be found at an LDS Home Storage Center, such as the leavening agents and fats, both of which you'll need to purchase elsewhere. You might also notice that it's not a complete list of foods to stockpile either, hence, why we have the original list of pantry foods discussed already. Last, the water amount shown is considered enough for two weeks as they state it's not practical to store more, though I disagree.

Now, the online calculator doesn't specifically state how to breakdown the pounds of food other than to do so via the major categories as shown above. Honestly, I don't have a better suggestion myself other than to say that it's up to you what to stockpile and how much.

Your family may, for instance, simply despise any meals with beans in it, but they love rice. Therefore, if I suggest you include more beans than rice in your food storage, then this may not work for you. Moreover, someone in your family may have allergies which then precludes you from stockpiling it, such as to wheat. So, again, what you need to stockpile will be specific to your needs and tastes.

The 5 Main Bulk Foods to Stockpile

Despite my hesitancy as noted above, and assuming you have no special dietary needs or taste preference, then I would focus on the following:

1. White rice (brown rice could be stored instead, if you prefer)
2. Macaroni (boxed macaroni would be an easier alternative for some meals)

3. Spaghetti (be sure to include pasta sauce, as mentioned previously)
4. Oats (regular is preferred, though instant oats would suffice)
5. Beans (black, pinto, great northern, and refried are all good to include)

The first three—white rice, macaroni, and spaghetti—are going to be your main meal fillers or bulk foods upon which you base a meal. As such, you're going to want to include plenty of them, although a little does tend to go a long way as a meal filler.

The oats are another great bulk food to add, especially since they make a welcome and warm breakfast food. No doubt, oats can be cooked and added to a variety of meals as a filler too.

Beans are good to include as well, though you should be aware that they take more work to prepare because dry beans need to be soaked before being cooked, will use more water because of this, and take longer to cook than either rice or pasta. FYI, I once wrote up a blog post on ten tips on how to cook dry beans that you may want to familiarize yourself with if you've never tried to cook with dry beans before.[23]

The refried beans are a nice side dish to have and taste rather good. The only drawback is that they don't tend to last for more than a handful of years in storage.

Should You Include Wheat or Flour?

Wheat is something we need to talk about. Oftentimes, people suggest you stockpile a lot of wheat, both red and white, for baking purposes. While I don't necessarily disagree, the entire reason for doing so is to turn that wheat into flour so that you can then make bread and other flour-necessary foods.

Unfortunately, turning wheat into flour is a lot of work, particularly without an electric grain mill to do the hard work.[24] If disaster strikes and the power goes out, then you really do need a good manual grinder to make this idea useful, such as the Wonder Junior Deluxe, which is what I own and use.[25]

Moreover, all the work involved in making bread from scratch may not be worthwhile in a short-term survival situation. As such, if you're intending on preparing for a short time of a few weeks, let's say, then stockpiling wheat to make flour and thus bread may not be the best plan. In a longer-term situation, on the other hand, you may very well want to stockpile wheat to make breads and whatnot, and I'd encourage doing so.

Of course, bread doesn't necessarily need to be leavened like we're accustomed to. You could, for instance, make a 30 second flat bread which I wrote about years ago.[26] In this case, stockpiling flour would be a far easier option, though you should know that flour tends not to last for more than a handful of years after being processed, even when properly stored.

6 Additional Bulk Foods to Include

The rest of the foods on the Cannery list are great to include as well, but should be considered secondary, in my opinion, to the main five foods I mentioned already, especially if you're just starting out or really need to stick to a budget.

As money and time permit, I would also include the following:

- Potato flakes (not the instant potatoes, mashed potato mix would be an alternative)
- Pancake mix (another great breakfast meal besides oats)
- Granola (for breakfast or even as a snack)
- Berry drink mix (to give you something sweet to drink)
- Cocoa mix (another drink alternative)
- Nonfat dry milk (for a variety of purposes)

Truth be told, the above list is mostly about giving your taste buds something else to enjoy, especially the drink mixes. Again, the main drawback is that the berry drink mix, cocoa mix, pancake mix, and granola have a short shelf life of less than a few years. Oddly enough, the milk is expected to last for up to twenty years.

The Remaining Foods

The final handful of options not yet discussed on the list of Home Storage Center foods are all fine to include as well, if you like. The apple slices, for example, would be a welcome treat, while the carrots and onions could be added to some meals and will offer added nutrition.

Finally, the sugar and honey could both be used as sweeteners and for baking purposes, while the peanut butter may find use as a snack. In any event, I wouldn't spend a lot of money on these remaining foods.

How to Store Bulk Foods

Although there are different methods of storing bulk foods for years, even decades, by far the easiest way is to use Mylar bags and oxygen absorbers, both of which come in various sizes depending on your needs. Just search Amazon for *Mylar food storage bags* and *oxygen absorbers* and you'll find plenty of options, even those that conveniently pair an appropriately sized oxygen absorber with a Mylar bag, which is certainly the easiest choice.

Use this resource to determine how to match Mylar bag size with oxygen absorber capacity if you need help and this website reference shows you how to use Mylar bags for food storage.[27,28]

In any case, the most common size of Mylar bags for food storage you'll encounter are one-gallon and five-gallon bags. The five-gallon bags are great if you're wanting to store large quantities of a single food, such as wheat or rice, in a five- or six-gallon bucket. The one-gallon bags are better for storing food in smaller containers or for including more than one type of food in a single bucket. I do both, though I tend to prefer to stockpile smaller quantities in one-gallon bags rather than storing only one type of food in a single bucket.

Although some folks prefer using FDA food-grade buckets so you don't have to use Mylar bags (it's the white bucket on the far left shown in the photo below) I've also used plenty of non-food-grade buckets with Mylar bags which can be purchased for only a few dollars at most any hardware store, such as these orange buckets I bought at Home Depot many years ago:

To be clear: The orange buckets are not suitable to be used without a Mylar bag protecting the bucket from leeching chemical contaminants into your food. The white bucket, on the other hand, is an FDA food-grade bucket, not because it's white, but because it's designed to not leech chemicals. That's a nice benefit, but you will pay a price for these buckets.

Personally, I use the food-grade buckets for storing several bulk foods that I want easy access to, including flour, beans, and noodles; I then use gamma seal lids for easy access.[29] You don't have to go that far with bulk foods, though it does make using them on a regular basis significantly easier. Even stores like Walmart are beginning to carry the gamma seal lids and food storage buckets, so check around if that interests you.

In any case, I would strongly encourage you to properly label and date each bucket so that you know what's contained within, as I've done here:

The label might be a bit difficult to read from the photo above, but it states that I have one each of pasta, red wheat, white rice, and two rolled oats contained within. The label also states that I packed this bucket in March 2009.

You don't have to get this fancy. Simply write the date and contents on the bucket with permanent marker and that will suffice, and don't write on the lid in case they get misplaced after opening.

Here's an example of the rolled oats I had stored in that bucket, still neatly packaged in a one-gallon Mylar bag:

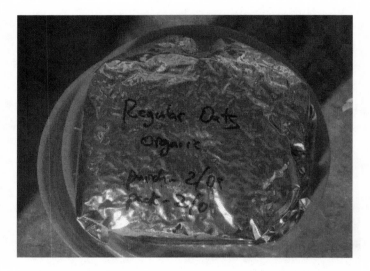

Sometimes the oxygen absorber seems to suck in the bag and form around the contents, other times it doesn't. So long as the bag is clearly still sealed, the food should be fine. You do need to be careful with some foods such as spaghetti noodles, since they can poke a hole in the Mylar bag, thereby allowing air to enter during the initial packaging process.

For foods which may pose such a risk, look for thicker Mylar bags (usually 5 mil thickness) so they can stand up to the abuse. Most other foods, such as oats, beans, rice, and certainly flour, can be packaged in most any Mylar bag.

One last caution: Ensure the buckets you buy have a rubber seal in the lid. This will help to keep oxygen and water from intruding and will further protect your bulk foods if, for example, a bag ended up getting a hole, and you didn't realize it.

Food packaged in #10 cans should already have an appropriate oxygen absorber included inside. Here's an example of how food comes from the LDS Home Storage Center. Some of it was prepackaged by them and some was done by me at their cannery:

The Home Storage Centers always provide nutrition labels, though I tend to write dates purchased on the outside of the box as well. FYI, there are always six #10 cans to a case when you purchase from the Home Storage Center which, to be clear, is the easiest and cheapest way to buy and store the aforementioned bulk foods I recommend.

Bulk Foods Recap

If I haven't made this clear yet, you can't beat the local LDS Home Storage Center for bulk foods pricing, particularly when you add in the cost of shipping and repackaging for long-term storage. If you have a nearby Home Storage Center, then please make use of it!

After all, you can purchase a wide range of bulk foods at a very low cost, everything from rice and beans, to wheat, pasta, and even a few vegetables and fruit, all properly packaged for long-term storage. Now, if for some reason you don't want to visit a nearby Home Storage Center, then you can always make a purchase online, though you'll pay a bit more for the same foods and a minimal amount for shipping.

Remember, too, that you do not need to be a member of the church. They're more than happy to sell you food but may limit what you can purchase at any one time. Last, the folks who run these facilities are volunteers, so please be nice and respect their rules and their way of doing things. Everyone I've ever met at the Home Storage Centers has been very nice and helpful.

Ultimately, it's a win-win for you and them because you're getting good food at a great price and they get to sell it to you. Take advantage of this wonderful resource while you can.

Some final considerations:

1. Realize that not all bulk foods can be stored for decades. Some foods, such as flour and drink mixes, for instance, may only be viable for a few years.
2. Storage temperatures and even humidity, too, make a difference in length of storage; consider where you might keep these foods for longevity purposes.
3. As you continue to purchase bulk foods, be sure to rotate cans so that you use the oldest food first. Doing so will ensure your bulk foods stay as fresh as possible even though they're packaged to last for many years to come.
4. Consider keeping a spreadsheet or other tally sheet so you know what you have at any one time. This will also help you realize when you may need to purchase more.
5. Try to use these bulk foods regularly so that you know how to use them and so that you become accustomed to eating them in your daily meals.

Remember that bulk foods are great to add as a calorie supplement or filler to your existing food supply and should never be your only food source.

Finally, I should mention that you don't necessarily have to stockpile such large amounts of dry food for emergencies. You could, alternatively, buy smaller bags of the essentials—rice, beans, pasta, oats—from the grocery store, if you prefer. Personally, I'd rather have more food than not; you'll have to decide what's right for your situation.

19 Shelf-Stable Superfoods to Stockpile

When I originally had the idea for this book, I wanted to only compile a list of typical shelf-stable foods one would find at the local grocery store in order to maximize nutrition. I realized, however, that even more could be done to supplement and to maximize your body's nutritional needs with superfoods.

These foods are often high in a variety of nutrients which, besides calories, are vital to your health. I should emphasize that this list of supplements should not be considered replacements for the everyday pantry foods or bulk foods already discussed.

That is, in most cases these superfoods cannot and will not provide all your body's dietary needs for the simple fact that they do not contain enough of any one specific requirement, such as protein or fiber, and so they shouldn't be relied upon alone; all superfoods listed herein are supplements and should be treated as such.

With that in mind, this book wouldn't be complete without adding to what we've discussed thus far with a variety of additional options you might consider adding to your preps and maybe even for use now to enhance your own health.

Of course, I'm not a doctor or healthcare professional. Thus, my recommendations shouldn't be taken as gospel. Realize, too, that whatever you choose to add to your diet and preparations should first be consulted with by a knowledgeable healthcare provider, dietician, or doctor. After all, I don't know your health situation and it's possible that some of these recommendations could be contraindicated for your health needs for some reason I can't foresee or don't understand.

With that out of the way, my purpose in the following recommendations is to add yet another layer to your food preparations, thereby bolstering your health and hopefully making things a bit easier when times get tough. My reasoning is threefold:

1. Although you may be consuming a variety of foods, you may not be properly digesting every vitamin and mineral your body needs due to increased stress levels or a significant change in diet, such as eating a large portion of bulk foods that you normally don't eat.

2. If you've consumed most of your pantry foods and you're now down to only the basics of rice and beans, for example, you're going to want a way to add at least some nutrients that are assuredly lacking; these superfoods are a potential way to do that.

3. Moving a lot of canned and packaged goods (such as during a bug out) may not be feasible, though moving a bit of canned goods and adding smaller containers of superfoods could be. Again, don't rely solely on these supplemental superfoods.

I should also mention that most, if not all, of the following superfoods are shelf-stable or, at the very least, do not need refrigeration, though it's quite possible that I've missed something or that you might purchase a similar product to which I recommend that requires refrigeration. As such, please perform your own due diligence to ensure that whatever you purchase doesn't need to be refrigerated until being opened or, better yet, not at all.

That said, I have run into supplements in the past which suggest refrigeration after opening, yet don't really need it, especially if you're going to be using it up in short order. Again, do you research before making any assumptions as to a food's shelf-stability and refrigeration needs.

No doubt, likely every supplement included will have an expiration date. These usually aren't strict requirements but, rather, guidelines and will vary greatly depending on storage conditions. Therefore, it's quite possible that most every superfood included will stay good for a significant time past the expiration date listed.

Of course, there are many factors involved in how long a supplement might be viable. Typically, solids will stay viable for longer than powders and powders longer than liquids. Because of this, I try to avoid liquids if there are powders available and you should, too.

Last, keep these supplements out of the light and away from high temperatures and, in some cases, freezing temperatures as well. It might even be best to package them like any other long-term food storage item, that is, in Mylar bags and with oxygen absorbers to lengthen viability. I don't personally do this, but I know of some folks who do, and they believe it works.

Now, with regards to the following list, I've broken it down into three main categories:

1. Superfoods to boost nutrition;
2. Superfoods to aid with digestion and immune support;
3. Superfoods that didn't fit elsewhere.

I began the list with foods that can be used to increase vitamins and minerals to ensure your body is working at an optimal level, even during a disaster. I then continued with a few superfoods that may aid with your digestive health because stress and a change in diet can become a real problem during a disaster. Finally, we end this discussion with a handful of superfoods that may prove useful to you, yet didn't seem to fit elsewhere.

Superfoods to Boost Nutrition

I would strongly encourage you to include as many of the following nutritional foods in your pantry as possible, since they'll help to boost a wide variety of critical vitamins and minerals that may be difficult to come by with food alone.

Quality Multivitamin

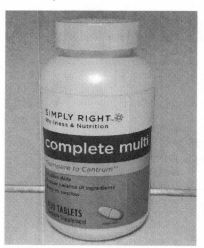

You should include a quality multivitamin as a stop-gap for any vitamin or mineral deficiency you may have in your diet. Granted, some vitamins or minerals are needed in minute quantities, but if you're not getting them from the foods you'd normally be consuming because they're unavailable, then a multivitamin may be the only source.

Because there are literally so many options available on the market, I'm not going to attempt to recommend one option over another. I will say, that you should ensure the supplement you choose includes as many of the vitamins and minerals on this list as possible and in appropriate quantities to your age and gender since there are differences we need to consider, and look for a supplement that's a solid pill, if possible, as these will tend to store the longest.[30]

Last, I'm told that whatever vitamin you take, test it to see that it will breakdown in water within five minutes. There are several vitamins that go through the body and are eliminated without breaking down. Interesting, I need to give that a try.

Liquid Minerals (or multivitamins)

There are a wide variety of shelf-stable liquid vitamins worth exploring if, let's say, you know you have a specific need. For example, living in the Pacific Northwest, we don't get much sunlight during the winter and my wife insists we take a liquid vitamin D supplement to make up for any deficiencies.[31] My wife also likes our children to occasionally take this BodyBio Premixed Liquid Minerals for their teeth.[32]

Bear in mind that magnesium is important to store. Your body uses it in over 500 different things to keep your body going. Our foods are depleted from the minerals we need. Therefore, you are not getting the magnesium you need.

There plenty of other options and even liquid multivitamins, if interested. Why bother? After all, I did just mention that liquids tend to not last as long as powders or solids. Well, it seems that liquid vitamins require less effort to breakdown for absorption which, if times are stressful, could prove more useful than a pill since your body wouldn't have to do as much work in order to get the needed benefits.

Additionally, most liquid vitamins are shelf-stable and quite potent, which makes them perfect for a disaster situation. A major drawback is that a liquid vitamin or mineral supplement simply won't last nearly as along as a pill or powder, as stated earlier. If it's something you'll take regularly now, then I would encourage you to store an extra bottle or two, so you always have what you need on hand.

Eggs: Real or Freeze-Dried

In my humble opinion, I consider eggs a superfood in their own right since they're high in protein and omega-3 fats, include a variety of vitamins and minerals—here's a good reference—such as all the B-vitamins and even include disease-fighting nutrients like lutein.[33]

Although the best way to keep eggs viable is in a hen or, barring that, refrigerated, you can also store eggs for months without refrigeration by coating them with mineral oil. I've done this myself and the eggs outlasted my multi-month experiment! (FYI, here's my final week's experiment recap, if interested.[34])

For that experiment, I also kept some eggs uncoated and out of refrigeration as a control group and many of them lasted for several weeks without worry, though I began to wonder about their edibility near the end of the eighteen-week ordeal. If you plan on using this idea to keep eggs, then you should know how to tell if an egg is good or bad so you don't get sick.[35]

Of course, even coating eggs and using the float test is not ideal. To store eggs for many months, even several years, you should consider freeze-dried whole egg powder or scrambled egg mix, such as this #10 can by Augason Farms.[36]

Be aware that you can also purchase powdered egg whites which you don't want because most of the nutrients are in the yolk. Realize, too, that some powdered eggs sold online are packaged in bags which won't store as well as in #10 cans. I've also seen places like Walmart sell freeze-dried foods, which may be an even cheaper way to stock up on powdered eggs and more. Finally, freeze-dried foods shouldn't need to be refrigerated after opening either, merely used within a reasonable timeframe of about one year for most products.

Chia Seeds

I'm a big fan of these little seeds because, pound-for-pound, they're a powerhouse of nutrition, including protein, omega-3 fats, lots of fiber, calcium, as well as other vitamins and minerals.

In fact, according to this article on chia seeds, "The chia seed is nutrient dense and packs a punch of energy-boosting power. Aztec warriors ate chia seeds to give them energy and endurance, claiming that just one spoonful of chia could sustain them for 24 hours. Chia means 'strength' in the Mayan language, and chia seeds were known as 'runners' food' because runners and warriors would use them as fuel while running long distances or during battle."[37]

I don't know how true that claim is, though I can say that chia seeds are the type of food which can be added to almost anything eaten in a bowl, such as soups to stews, and you'll never even notice them. Personally, I like to add chia seeds to my occasional morning yogurt or oatmeal, and I've been known to toss them into soups too. Moreover, the above referenced article discusses soaking the seeds to release enzyme inhibitors, but I've never tried that and have always consumed them raw.

There are plenty of sellers out there and, honestly, I can't tell the difference between one over the other. That said, I have purchased this Viva brand chia seeds multiple times.[38]

Flax Seeds

Flax seeds are very much like chia seeds in that they're small and pound-for-pound pack a nutritional punch for your health. Just like with chia seeds, flax seeds are relatively high in protein, fiber, omega-3 fats, as well as a variety of vitamins, such as vitamin E and some B vitamins, and even include antioxidants.

About the only major difference I've found is that flax seeds provide a source of choline for your brain that chia seeds do not, whereas chia seeds offer more iron, calcium, and selenium than flax seeds do. For this reason, it may be wise to add small amounts of both seeds to your meals.

Be aware that flax seeds tend to go rancid faster than chia seeds will due to a higher fat content. Both types of seeds can be stored in the refrigerator to slow down this process, but it's not necessary if consumed in a reasonable period.

Last, flax seeds can be purchased as either a whole kernel or already ground. While the whole kernel will store longer, it's my understanding that, unlike chia seeds, flax seeds must be ground for better absorption of nutrients, especially the fats. You must, therefore, be able to grind the flax seeds into a powder to maximize nutritional yield. This should be easy enough to do with a coffee grinder. Of course, you'll need a power source to make that happen or you'll need to invest in a mortar and pestle and some elbow grease when the power goes out.

Coconut Oil

I must admit that I'm not a fan of anything with coconut and that includes coconut oil. There's just something about the texture which I detest. Regardless, I put up with it because I believe the health benefits of coconut oil outweigh my general distaste for it.

Coconut oil is basically 100% fat, most of which is considered the bad sort of fat, specifically saturated fat. That said, it appears the saturated fats in coconut oil are different than those typically found in animal fats, which makes them healthier options, according to this article.[39]

Realize, too, that not all coconut oils are created equal. Basically, you want virgin coconut oil, not partially hydrogenated or refined oils. This is important! And if you can buy organic, then all the better. Personally, we buy the Kirkland brand organic virgin coconut oil from Costco.[40]

Fortunately, a little bit goes a long way. One big jar like the one pictured above will also last for many months, even years, depending on use. Realize, too, that coconut oil is a solid at room temperature but will quickly liquefy at temperatures slightly above that; it's nothing to worry about as it will solidify again at room temperature or below and can be used, regardless.

While you can certainly include coconut oil into your diet by eating it plain or adding to soups—my wife used to add it to our morning smoothies. You can also use it in place of vegetable or olive oils for cooking, thereby adding good fats to your diet without any effort.

Moreover, while I'm a bit skeptical of all the touted uses, people apparently use coconut oil for a variety of reasons, including for skin care, hair care, dental care, and even to aid with digestion, as well as plenty of other potential uses.[41] The most important reason to include it, in this case, is for use as a substitute cooking oil.

Spirulina

Spirulina is a "marine superfood" made from blue-green algae...pond scum, as I've seen it described. It, like many products out there, is touted as possibly aiding a wide range of ailments. No doubt more study is necessary, but what isn't disputed is the nutritional aspects. For starters, spirulina is about 60-70% protein by weight. It includes a significant amount of calcium, niacin, potassium, magnesium, iron, and B vitamins, and is loaded with antioxidants.

Like many of the aforementioned foods, a little goes a long way. A single teaspoon of the powder we use is a suggested serving.[42] There are spirulina pills, if you prefer, which also do not need refrigeration, though I've not used them.[43]

Alternative: Chlorella

Chlorella is yet one more marine superfood seaweed algae, very similar to spirulina. It's very high in vitamin A, protein, iron, riboflavin, zinc, as well as a variety of other nutrients, and apparently has a significant cleansing effect on the body according to some.[44]

The powder form is recommended to be refrigerated, though I've seen products which don't require it. Stored in a cool, dry, dark place, even the powder should stay viable for many months or even years. I won't bother to recommend anything as it's been quite a while since we've purchased a chlorella supplement; a simple Amazon search will yield plenty of options, both powders and pills, to choose from.

Protein Powder

There isn't much I can elaborate on with regards to protein powder since it's literally just a protein supplement. Usually marketed to the exercise enthusiasts—specifically the muscle building community—a quality whey protein powder could be just the supplement you've been looking for to ensure your body gets all the protein it needs.

After all, protein plays a major role in a healthy body as this webmd.com article points out: "Protein is an important component of every cell in the body. Hair and nails are mostly made of protein. Your body uses protein to build and repair tissues. You also use protein to make enzymes, hormones, and other body chemicals. Protein is an important building block of bones, muscles, cartilage, skin, and blood. Along with fat and carbohydrates, protein is a 'macronutrient,' meaning that the body needs relatively large amounts of it. Vitamins and minerals, which are needed in only small quantities, are called 'micronutrients.' But unlike fat and carbohydrates, the body does not store protein, and therefore has no reservoir to draw on when it needs a new supply."[45]

I'd say that makes getting enough protein from our foods important, wouldn't you? Spend any time researching and you'll find that there are plenty of choices out there, so it's hard to recommend one specific brand. I will suggest that you want a protein powder which is high in essential amino acids and readily absorbed, such as the MRM Veggie Protein Powder we have; the rest doesn't matter much unless you have a very specific need like avoiding allergens or trying to bulk up to elite bodybuilder status.[46] Personally, I've also stocked creatine powder as well since it has similar effects to whey protein powder, though, they are technically different as this article rightly points out.[47]

Wheat Germ

According to this Mayo Clinic article, wheat germ is one of the 10 great health foods.[48] The article states, "Wheat germ is the part of the grain that's responsible for the development and growth of the new plant sprout. Although only a small part, the germ contains many nutrients. It's an excellent source of thiamin and a good source of folate, magnesium, phosphorus and zinc. The germ also contains protein, fiber and some fat. Try sprinkling some on your hot or cold cereal."

Although most packaging says it's best to refrigerate after opening, wheat germ is probably shelf-stable at room temperature if you use it within a few months. Like many other nutritional superfoods mentioned thus far, wheat germ can be sprinkled into or on almost anything, since it has a relatively bland taste.

Cacao Powder

 Cacao powder is very bitter and I'm positive most people wouldn't enjoy it without adding a sweetener in some way. With that in mind, this article suggests you can make hot chocolate and even a raw brownie with it.[49] Personally, I've used it to make an impromptu hot chocolate with honey added as a sweetener and it wasn't too bad. In any case, cacao powder is full of antioxidants, iron, magnesium, and calcium, all minerals your body needs to stay healthy, and it may be the tastiest superfood of them all, with some honey added, that is.

Superfoods to Aid Digestion and Immune Support

Although the superfoods discussed thus far have been intended to provide you with extra nutrients, I would be remiss if I didn't also mention a few which may be helpful to your overall health, particularly for digestion and immune support.

Probiotics / Water Kefir Grains

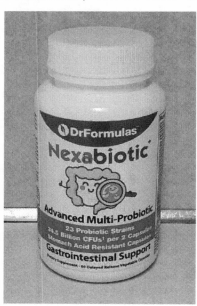

It seems to me that more evidence emerges each year as to how important gut bacteria are to a healthy digestive tract, including for two big reasons (1) to boost your immune system so you remain healthy and (2) improve digestion and, thus, your ability to absorb nutrients.

In my opinion, if you can take something that will decrease the likelihood of being sick and aid with maximizing nutrition, then it's a win-win! And that's precisely what probiotics are, beneficial gut bacteria that help to improve digestion and even boost your immune system.

The problem with many manufactured probiotics is that they tend to require refrigeration. There are some that don't require refrigeration such as these Nexabiotic Multi Probiotic supplements that I like to take once a day.[50]

Another option that doesn't require refrigeration and which I've had some experience with is water kefir grains. If you're heard of milk kefir, then they're essentially the same thing, but don't prefer milk to grow. Instead, they just need a sugary water solution to make their probiotic-goodness, which is great because sugar is shelf-stable.

Obviously, the only drawback here is that you'd need to replenish the sugar or stockpile plenty for this purpose. Fortunately, you only need about one cup of sugar for each gallon of water kefir, so it's not a lot of sugar to be used for each batch. Also, since the type of sugar you use doesn't seem to matter much, you can buy bulk sugar cheap and be set for years.

On another positive note, the water kefir grains will multiply over time, which means you could end up with more grains than you know what to do with.

I've tried a few different water kefir grains in the past and they seem to be about the same quality. Lately,

I've ordered these (you only need ¼ cup to start with) though I should point out that I tend to have trouble with growing them where I live during the colder winter months.[51]

Digestive Enzymes

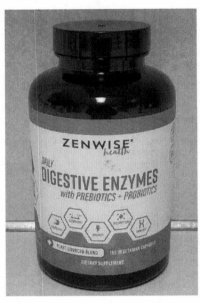

Sometimes your body needs help, even beyond what probiotics might be able to do. In this case, digestive enzymes may be just the thing. Be aware that digestive enzymes are often specific to an intended purpose. As such, you'll find enzymes for digesting fat, others for carbohydrates, ones for protein, and so on.

Fortunately, there are enzyme supplements which help with digesting more than one type of substance, if interested, such as these Zenwise Digestive Enzymes that my wife and I like to take with meals.[52] These digestive enzymes also include prebiotics and probiotics, which make them even more beneficial.

In my opinion, if you're digesting your food well now, then I wouldn't bother with adding a digestive enzyme supplement unless you currently have a reason for doing so.

Vitamin C Powder

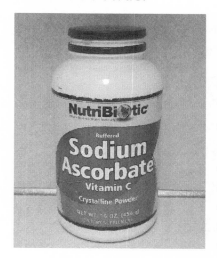

If there's one vitamin supplement which may be of more benefit to your health than almost any other, it's vitamin C, in my opinion. After all, scurvy is no joke and is a direct result of a lack of vitamin C, usually found in fresh fruits and vegetables, precisely the foods you'll be lacking as time goes on.

This Webmd.com article states, "Vitamin C is one of the safest and most effective nutrients, experts say. It may not be the cure for the common cold, though it's thought to help prevent more serious complications. But the benefits of vitamin C may include protection against immune system deficiencies, cardiovascular disease, prenatal health problems, eye disease, and even skin wrinkling [and that] '...higher blood levels of vitamin C may be the ideal nutrition marker for overall health."[53]

My research suggests that you should look for a buffered vitamin C powder in the form of sodium ascorbate rather than ascorbic acid because the body can apparently utilize that form better. I've used this NutriBiotic Sodium Ascorbate Vitamin C powder for quite a while and am pleased with it, especially how long it lasts.[54]

Fiber Powder or Psyllium Husk Powder

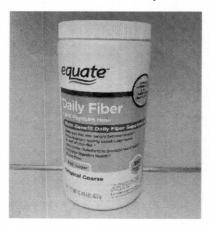

Besides properly digesting your food, being able to eliminate the waste produced is equally important. Psyllium husk powder is a soluble fiber that adds bulk to your stool, thereby allowing you to pass it better.

According to this article, psyllium husk powder can relieve diarrhea, which could be useful during stressful times, lower cholesterol, help manage blood sugar, and more.[55]

My interest in psyllium husk powder is solely with keeping your bowel movements regular. This Viva husk powder would be a good choice, though I don't see much difference between that and the store brand I have.[56] In any case, I would encourage you to further package it to keep the powder viable for longer, such as in food storage bags, and out of harsh temperatures.

Superfoods That Didn't Fit Elsewhere

Following are a few more supplement suggestions worth considering. The thing is that they don't quite fit in either of the aforementioned superfoods categories and, thus, ended up here. Nonetheless, they're still good for you to consider adding to your stockpile.

Green Tea

While not quite a nutrient-packed food per se, according to this article green tea, in particular, can aid with all sorts of health problems, including diabetes, some cancers, heart disease, cholesterol, blood pressure, and plenty more.[57] It's not just green tea, apparently a variety of teas have many potential health benefits. Personally, we keep quite a few different teas on hand, many of which simply taste good to us.

There are teas, however, which serve very specific purposes. For example, we have one tea that's meant to aid with bowel movements, and I can attest that it works quite well when you're backed up! There are other teas my wife likes to use for other problems that I cannot speak for. The point is that if you have a specific health problem, then there's likely a tea for that.

At the very least, adding a variety of teas makes for a welcome and warm beverage when water may typically be the only option you have.

Apple Cider Vinegar

 Have you ever tried to drink apple cider vinegar straight? It's horrible! And difficult to do at times, if you ask me. That said, I've been taking a tablespoon straight each morning to help with assorted aches and pains and it seems to be helping. You could, alternatively, dilute it in a cup of water to help mask the taste.

Regardless of my reasons, it might be worthwhile to add apple cider vinegar to your diet since it can help to regulate blood sugar levels, enhance weight loss, lower cholesterol, improve skin health, reduce blood pressure, and relieve symptoms of acid reflux, according to this article.[58]

The referenced article goes on to state that apple cider vinegar can be used to soothe a sunburn (I've never tried that personally and it sounds horrible), can be a natural deodorant (now we're getting crazy), reduce or remove warts (something we have tried on our children with success), and plenty more ways you might be interested to know about.

Fish Oil / Omega 3

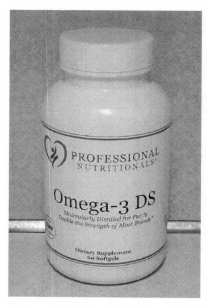

This article states that fish oil is another wondrous superfood to make use of: "The health benefits of fish oil include its ability to aid in weight loss and healthy pregnancy. It also promotes fertility and skin care (particularly for psoriasis and acne). It is beneficial in the treatment of various heart diseases, high cholesterol, depression, anxiety,

ADHD, weak immune system, diabetes, inflammation, arthritis, IBD, Alzheimer's disease, eye disorders, macular degeneration, and ulcers."[59]

Usually, fish oil or Omega 3 capsules don't require refrigeration, though it is recommended for some brands, so you'll need to keep an eye out for that.

The fish oil I prefer, Nordic Natural Omega 3, needs to be refrigerated after use, though, I also keep pills on hand as a backup.[60]

Raw Honey

Raw honey seems to have quite a few health benefits, including being a good source of antioxidants, has both antibacterial and antifungal properties, potentially heals wounds, helps with digestive issues, and more, as this article suggests.[61] There are many dozens more possible uses for honey, according to this website.[62]

The problem, it seems, is that you need a specific brand of raw honey for many of the potential health benefits, not just any store-bought honey you can find at the grocery store.[63] For that reason, I won't say honey can do everything some folks claim it can.

Regardless, honey is certainly a healthier sugar substitute and can be used for baking, or even in place of granulated sugar, in some cases. I've used it for baking purpose, such as when making homemade banana bread, and I'll use it in my yogurt or oatmeal to make it sweeter, among other uses as a sugar substitute.[64] Plus, it's twice as sweet as granulated sugars so you only need to use half as much for the same amount of sweetening.

Besides maple syrup, honey is probably the best natural sweetener you can get. It lasts nearly forever (it's been found in King Tut's tomb) and goes with or in almost anything that needs to be sweetened. Stock plenty.

Superfoods Recap

Obviously, there are many superfoods to choose from, so how do you? Personally, I wouldn't bother to stockpile every superfood listed if you don't already have a specific reason to keep something on hand as that would be too much and even redundant in some cases as well.

That said, remember the purpose of most of these superfoods is to act as yet another layer of nutrition to ensure you're as healthy as you can be when times get tough. Remember, too, that these supplements aren't replacements and shouldn't be treated as such, so don't rely on them solely for your nutritional needs.

Now, while it's entirely up to you as to what you stockpile, my recommendation would be to include a quality solid-pill multivitamin for sure, followed very closed by one or two powerhouse superfoods, such as chia seeds or spirulina. I would then also add in a protein powder and coconut oil to ensure your body has plenty of the two things it cannot make, yet desperately needs—protein and fat. I might also choose to include the fiber powder to aid with digestion during stressful times and, because I love probiotics and honey as a sweetener, I would add them as well.

Like I said, it's up to you what to include. Hopefully, there are enough options here for you to find supplements that work for you and your preferences. Depending on your situation and dietary needs, you may find that you don't need to take every supplement daily. For instance, you might only choose to use the chia seeds or spirulina occasionally, whereas you take a multivitamin daily. The fiber may only be needed for some meals and not others, and the honey may only find occasional use. You get the idea.

And, again, be sure to purchase superfoods which are shelf-stable when opened so you don't have to worry about refrigeration during a grid-down situation. Last, check with your healthcare professional to ensure any new supplements you intend to purchase are ok for you and your family to make use of.

How to Make Use of Everything

Now that you have all these wonderful shelf-stable pantry foods stored away, including dozens of bulk foods as well as a variety of superfoods, the next obvious question is: How can you make use of it all? Here's briefly what I think.

The bulk foods (e.g., rice, beans, noodles, etc.) are your meal fillers or they're the basis of meals. That is, you would either choose to add some rice, for instance, to a can of soup as a calorie filler or you base a meal on rice and add other foods to it, such as a can of green beans and tomatoes to give the meal flavor and some nutrition. The same can be said for several other dry foods, including beans, pasta, and even oats to a lesser degree.

Realize, though, that all bulk foods need water to be rehydrated and cooked; the amount of water needed will add up quickly! While it may seem to be a lot of work simply to add a bit of rice or noodles to a can of soup, when it comes down to making use of the only food you have when you cannot resupply for an extended period, a bit of extra work may be the only option you have. Furthermore, this strategy also means that you can stretch out the nutritional grocery store foods for as long as possible.

To make up for any nutritional deficiencies from relying largely on bulk foods, you might then add an appropriate superfood to these meals whenever possible. That is, you might add the chia seeds, flax seeds, or even spirulina and wheat germ to a meal right before you eat it since they tend to disappear into most foods, especially soups. The multivitamin, liquid minerals, vitamin C and fish oil could then be used for times when you don't cook something appropriate for the previously mentioned superfoods, or simply used as you prefer.

Moreover, the digestive enzymes and fiber powder can be used as needed, depending on your tolerance for various foods and elimination needs. Similarly, the coconut oil and honey have very specific uses that may or may not be of use regularly. The green tea (or any teas, for that matter) will likely be a welcome change of pace to drinking only water day after day unless, of course, you also choose to stockpile the bulk food drink mixes already discussed.

Last, the everyday pantry foods are the real nutritional and calorie powerhouses of everything discusses thus far. Although the bulk foods do add calories to your meals and the superfoods will increase many vitamins and minerals to an extent, it's the common grocery store canned and boxed foods which are vital to this overall strategy. It's these foods that you need to have in abundance. I would also encourage you to ensure you have a variety of seasonings and spices to give meals a variety of flavors, so you don't encounter appetite fatigue.

Final Thoughts

Here are a few more considerations I want to touch upon before we're done.

Food Combining for Nutrient Absorption

You should know that you can maximize the nutrients you get out of your food by combining the correct foods together. Legumes, such as beans and nuts, eaten with a grain provide a complete protein. For example, combine beans and rice or almond butter and wheat bread for best nutrient absorption. This webmd.com article provides several examples of food synergy, if interested.[65]

Water Revisited

Although this book is solely focused on food storage, you really do need to ensure you have plenty of water included in your survival plan—as well as the ability to procure and properly treat more—because it's so critical to life. After all, a person could survive for weeks or months on end without food (or, at least, very minimal food) but you won't last more than a few days without water.

And, like I pointed out earlier, bulk foods are all but useless without water to rehydrate them and to cook with. You will use a lot of water even beyond cooking and drinking needs, including an assortment of hygiene purposes, such as bathing, brushing your teeth, shaving, washing your hair, and definitely for washing your hands. Water is needed for cleaning dishes, clothes, household chores, supplies, and for certainly for cleaning wounds. Pets need water too!

Water is so important that you really cannot ignore it. My typical recommendation is to attempt to store at least a few gallons of water per person per day, with five gallons per person per day being a good number to aim for.

This is both very little water when compared to our normal everyday use and also a lot of water to actually store because water does take up quite a bit of space. A single 55-gallon water barrel, for instance, would only be enough to last one person for, let's say, ten days assuming you leave a bit of space for expansion and expect some loss due to mishap. To last a month, you would, therefore, need three barrels. A family of four would require twelve barrels. You get the idea.

Keep Up with Your Food Storage Regularly

It seems to me that we're never lucky enough to have a disaster strike the day after we go to the grocery store and have a fully stocked pantry. A disaster will, inevitably, strike the day before you intend to go grocery shopping or, at the very least, when you're least prepared for one overall.

This is why it's crucial to your survival that you really must keep up with all of your preparations, especially food storage, because you may not have sufficient warning to rush out and purchase what you need. As such, it behooves you to keep up with your food storage needs regularly.

And, while this can be difficult to do, I find that using a spreadsheet for some items (like bulk foods) helps me to realize when I need to restock. In addition, labels on pantry shelves also help me to realize what it is that I might be missing with a glance. And, of course, simply adding foods to a grocery list as you use them is a tried-and-true method of keeping track as well.

In any case, assuming nothing will happen until you're ready for it is a recipe for disasters to be worse than they need to be. It's why I ensure my vehicle's gas tank is always half full, why I keep my phone fully charged as often as possible, and why I insist on ensuring we have food and water stockpiled as much as I can. You should as well.

How Does the Author's Food Storage Stack Up?

I thought it would be interesting to share how my own food storage stacks up with regards to this very list. Here's where we stand, in no particular order.

We do keep some breakfast cereals always on hand, but they're not specifically fortified with any fiber or nutrients. We have plenty of canned foods in the pantry, especially a variety of canned beans and vegetables. We also keep some canned fish (mostly tuna fish) but we don't keep any canned meats because my wife isn't a big fan. I do tend to keep canned chili, chowder, and other soups in the pantry, each of which makes for ready to eat meals.

We also have some canned fruit because my youngest son likes it on occasion, but not that much. Truth be told, we do include freeze-dried fruit (and vegetables, by the way) in #10 cans; it's probably the best way to store fruits and vegetables for years.

I also store other foods discussed previously in freeze-dried form, including eggs, butter, milk, and plenty more because it's easily the most nutritious way to store these foods long-term. Look at your local grocery store for freeze-dried foods (my Walmart carries them) or go online and get what you can there, if interested. Just know that these foods will get expensive to purchase this way; the same can be said for canned meat.

I also have an assortment of seeds and nuts stored in vacuum-sealed mason jars, but we don't tend to get into them that often. Regardless, such foods will last for years stored like this, unless they go rancid due to a high oil content. Similarly, we do always keep a few jars of peanut butter, almond butter, mayonnaise, and other condiments not otherwise mentioned before in the pantry.

While we do buy and store some of the other snack foods, like cookies, crackers, potato chips, pretzels, hard candies, and so on, they don't tend to last long with my kids around, so I don't try very hard to keep all of these items on hand at all times.

I keep plenty of all the bulk foods discussed, with the exception of granola. I have nothing against granola—we do purchase smaller boxes from Costco. I just never bothered to buy any in bulk, which I probably should. We also keep plenty of the ingredients to make bread from scratch, as well as the ability to grind grain and bake bread without electricity. This would be a lot of work, though.

As the photos throughout indicate, I have all the nineteen superfoods discussed, so we're good there, and I ensure I purchase more well before we might run out.

We do keep plenty of an assortment of cooking oils, especially coconut oil and olive oil, jellies, seasonings—particularly salt and pepper—and I do hide my fair share of chocolates from the rest of the family.

Last, we don't stock much in the way of alternative drinks besides a wide variety of herbal teas, the powdered berry drink mix, some hot chocolate mix, and lemonade that I have stashed away somewhere. My wife and I aren't fans of canned juice of any sort (though I did get on a juice kick years ago) and we don't drink iced tea either.

That about covers it. Overall, I think we do fairly well and cover the vast majority of my recommendations, with a few purposeful exceptions.

How about you? How does your pantry stack up at the moment? Are there any glaring deficiencies or do you tend to have everything covered? And is there something you simply must have which isn't on the list?

No matter what you choose to include, be sure you keep on top of things as regularly as possible so that when disaster strikes, you're ready for it!

Get Your Free 57-Point Checklist Here

Before you grab your checklist, be a good friend or family member and choose to help others who could use this crucial information.

Spread the Word, Share the Knowledge

I'm willing to bet that you have family and friends who could benefit from this book as well, so please take a moment right now and quickly share a link to it on Facebook, Twitter, or Pinterest...you can easily do so here.[66]

Now, download your free, easy-to-reference 57 foods to stockpile checklist here.[67]

Discover More Survival Books Here

If you liked what you read within, then you're going to love my other survival books.[68] Here's a sampling, just click on any book title below to find out more or use the link provided above to see them all:

- *144 Survival Uses for 10 Common Items*[69]
- *27 Crucial Smartphone Apps for Survival*[70]
- *28 Powerful Home Security Solutions*[71]
- *47 Easy DIY Survival Projects*[72]
- *53 Essential Bug Out Bag Supplies*[73]
- *75 of the Best Secret Hiding Places*[74]
- *9.0 Cascadia Earthquake Survival*[75]
- *Small Space Prepping Solutions*[76]
- *The Complete Pet Safety Action Plan*[77]
- *The Survival Toolbox*[78]
- *Your Identity Theft Protection Game Plan*[79]

Recommended for You

I want to point out one book from the above list, in particular, since you now clearly recognize the importance of being prepared at home: *53 Essential Bug Out Bag Supplies: How to Build a Suburban "Go Bag" You Can Rely Upon*.

Sadly, most every bug out bag list has some unwritten expectation that you'll be evacuating into a plentiful nearby wilderness with fish to catch, streams to rest alongside, mountains to navigate, and debris huts to build.

This just isn't the case for most of us.

Most Americans are going to be slogging their way through the urban jungle with nothing to catch for food or even a good source of water to drink! There may even be potentially unrecognizable building and roads as well as a shortage of safe shelter spots to get out of the elements.

These juxtapositions in bug out environments are quite different and should be treated as such. Click here to discover precisely how to create a "go bag" you can rely upon in a suburban environment.[80]

Your Opinion Matters to Me

I'd love to hear your feedback about this book, especially anything I might be able to add or improve upon for future revisions. Please send an email to rethinksurvival@gmail.com with the word "book" in the subject if you have something for me. (And be sure to include the book title so I'm not confused.)

Review This Book on Amazon

Lastly, I ask that you take a moment and write a review of my book on Amazon.com so that others know what to expect, particularly if you've found my advice useful.[81] (Note: you'll be sent to Amazon.com to write the review after clicking this link.)

I do hope that you've enjoyed this book and that you will choose to implement my recommendations to help you and your family be as healthy as possible during the next big disaster.

I encourage you to please take a moment and download the 57-point checklist above, share this book with your friends and family using the link I provided previously, and leave a quick review on Amazon.com while you're at it.

May God bless you and your family.

Thank you for your time, Damian

Appendices

Appendix A: 57-Point Checklist

Appendix B: List of Resources

Appendix A

27 GROCERY STORE FOODS TO STOCKPILE

1. Breakfast cereals (fortified with fiber or vitamins; source of several macronutrients)
2. Canned beans (all types; good source of protein, fiber, and some vitamins)
3. Canned chili (alternative to soup; source of fiber)
4. Canned chowder (alternative to soup; source of fat)
5. Canned fish (all types; good source of protein and some vitamins and minerals)
6. Canned fruits (all types; major source of vitamins)
7. Canned meats (all types; good source of protein, carbs, and more)
8. Canned soups (all types; good way to mix a variety of nutritious foods)
9. Canned vegetables (all types; major source of vitamins)
10. Chocolates (required snack for many people; source of fat and calories)
11. Cookies (tasty snack; may include a variety of macronutrients)
12. Cooking oils, lard, butter (source of fiber, fat, calories)
13. Crackers (another snack; may be a good source of fat, fiber, and carbs)

14. Hard candies (all types; great for a carb boost and tasty treat for kids)
15. Ingredients to make bread (e.g., flour, salt, sugar, oil, yeast)
16. Iced tea (alternative drink; source of carbs)
17. Jelly (any kind; source of carbs)
18. Mayonnaise (will need refrigeration after opening; source of fat and calories)
19. Nuts and nut butters (raw is great, butters are good too; source of several macronutrients)
20. Pasta sauce (all types; needed for bulk spaghetti and macaroni)
21. Popcorn kernels (be sure to include cooking oil; source of fiber)
22. Potato chips (tasty snack; often a source of fiber, protein, and fat)
23. Pre-mixed canned drinks, such as V8 juice (alternative drink; includes vitamins)
24. Pretzels (tasty snack; source of carbs and fiber)
25. Seasonings (very useful to avoid appetite fatigue; stock plenty of options)
26. Seeds (raw is great and can be sprinkled in many meals; source of several macronutrients)
27. Sweetened powdered drink mix, such as lemonade or fruit drink (alternative drink)

11 BULK FOODS TO STOCKPILE

1. Beans (black, pinto, great northern, and refried are all good to include)

2. Berry drink mix (to give you something sweet to drink)
3. Cocoa mix (another drink alternative)
4. Granola (for breakfast or even as a snack)
5. Macaroni (boxed macaroni would be an easier alternative for some meals)
6. Nonfat dry milk (for a variety of purposes)
7. Oats (regular is preferred, though instant oats would suffice)
8. Pancake mix (another great breakfast meal besides oats)
9. Potato flakes (not the instant potatoes; mashed potato mix would be an alternative)
10. Spaghetti (be sure to include pasta sauce)
11. White rice (brown rice could be stored instead, if you prefer)

19 SUPERFOODS TO STOCKPILE

Superfoods to Boost Nutrition
1. Cacao powder (could be used for some baking needs, also as a chocolate drink; needs sweetened)
2. Chia seeds (bland taste can be sprinkled into almost anything)
3. Coconut oil (good fat to cook with)
4. Eggs (freeze dried stores for years, real eggs can be coated in mineral oil to last months)
5. Flax seeds (includes similar nutrients to chia seeds, but higher oil content may not store as well)

6. Liquid minerals or multivitamin (more easily digested than a pill, useful during times of stress)
7. Multivitamin (pill form will stay viable the longest)
8. Protein powder (adequate amounts of protein is very important to maintaining a healthy body)
9. Spirulina (powder is a good choice and can go with almost any soup or stew)
10. Chlorella (like spirulina)
11. Wheat germ (bland taste can be sprinkled into almost anything)

Superfoods to Aid Digestion and Immune Support
12. Digestive enzymes (helps to breakdown foods; could be beneficial during times of stress)
13. Fiber powder or psyllium husk powder (helps keep you regular; stress can cause digestive problems)
14. Probiotics or water kefir grains (useful for proper gut health)
15. Vitamin C powder (avoid scurvy and boosts your immune system)

Superfoods That Didn't Fit Anywhere Else
16. Apple cider vinegar (assorted health benefits as well as other possible uses)
17. Fish oil or omega 3 (assorted health benefits)
18. Green tea (or any tea you prefer, even teas that serve specific purposes)
19. Raw honey (nature's near perfect sweetener; lasts nearly forever)

Appendix B

- Link 1: https://rethinksurvival.com/books/food-storage-checklist.php
- Link 2: https://rethinksurvival.com/books/food-book-offer.php
- Link 3: https://rethinksurvival.com/kindle-books/
- Link 4: https://www.fda.gov/downloads/food/guidanceregulation/guidancedocumentsregulatoryinformation/labelingnutrition/ucm513817.pdf
- Link 5: https://www.fns.usda.gov/estimated-calorie-needs-day-age-gender-and-physical-activity-level
- Link 6: https://www.ars.usda.gov/northeast-area/beltsville-md-bhnrc/beltsville-human-nutrition-research-center/food-surveys-research-group/docs/fndds-download-databases/
- Link 7: https://www.ars.usda.gov/ARSUserFiles/80400530/apps/2015-2016 FNDDS At A Glance - FNDDS Nutrient Values.xlsx
- Link 8: http://www.webmd.com/food-recipes/guide/vitamins-and-minerals-good-food-sources

- Link 9: http://www.home-remedies-for-you.com/vitamins/b-complex-vitamins/food.html
- Link 10: http://www.webmd.com/food-recipes/guide/vitamins-and-minerals-good-food-sources
- Link 11: https://classic.lds.org/maps/
- Link 12: https://providentliving.lds.org/self-reliance/food-storage/home-storage-center-locations?lang=eng
- Link 13: https://providentliving.lds.org/self-reliance/food-storage/home-storage-center-locations?lang=eng
- Link 14: https://providentliving.lds.org/self-reliance/food-storage/home-storage-center-locations?lang=eng
- Link 15: https://providentliving.lds.org/bc/providentliving/content/english/self-reliance/food-storage/home-storage-center-order-form/pdf/HomeStorageCenterOrderForm-US-short.pdf?lang=eng
- Link 16: https://store.lds.org/SearchDisplay?categoryId=&storeId=10151&catalogId=3074457345616676768&langId=-1&sType=SimpleSearch&resultCatEntryType=2&showResultsPage=true&searchSource=Q&pageView=&beginIndex=0&pageSize=20&searchTerm=food+storage

- Link 17: http://www.bulkfoods.com/
- Link 18: https://www.costco.com/
- Link 19: https://allbulkfoods.com/
- Link 20: https://www.beprepared.com/
- Link 21: https://providentliving.lds.org/bc/providentliving/content/english/self-reliance/food-storage/home-storage-center-order-form/pdf/HomeStorageCenterOrderForm-US-short.pdf?lang=eng
- Link 22: https://providentliving.com/preparedness/food-storage/foodcalc/
- Link 23: https://rethinksurvival.com/10-tips-how-to-cook-dry-beans/
- Link 24: https://rethinksurvival.com/kindle-books/food-storage-recommends/#electric
- Link 25: https://rethinksurvival.com/kindle-books/food-storage-recommends/#manual
- Link 26: https://rethinksurvival.com/how-to-make-bread-in-30-seconds/
- Link 27: https://www.usaemergencysupply.com/information-center/packing-your-own-food-storage/oxygen-absorbers-recommended-amounts
- Link 28: https://www.backdoorsurvival.com/using-mylar-bags-for-food-storage/

- Link 29: https://rethinksurvival.com/kindle-books/food-storage-recommends/#gamma
- Link 30: https://www.precisionnutrition.com/all-about-vitamins-minerals
- Link 31: https://rethinksurvival.com/kindle-books/food-storage-recommends/#vitamind
- Link 32: https://rethinksurvival.com/kindle-books/food-storage-recommends/#minerals
- Link 33: http://www.whfoods.com/genpage.php?tname=foodspice&dbid=92
- Link 34: https://rethinksurvival.com/egg-storage-experiment-week-18-results-the-final-week/
- Link 35: https://food-hacks.wonderhowto.com/how-to/tell-if-your-expired-eggs-are-still-good-eat-0154309/
- Link 36: https://rethinksurvival.com/kindle-books/food-storage-recommends/#eggpowder
- Link 37: https://draxe.com/chia-seeds-benefits-side-effects/
- Link 38: https://rethinksurvival.com/kindle-books/food-storage-recommends/#chiaseeds
- Link 39: http://www.medicalnewstoday.com/articles/282857.php

- Link 40: https://rethinksurvival.com/kindle-books/food-storage-recommends/#coconut
- Link 41: https://www.organicfacts.net/health-benefits/oils/health-benefits-of-coconut-oil.html
- Link 42: https://rethinksurvival.com/kindle-books/food-storage-recommends/#spirulinapowder
- Link 43: https://rethinksurvival.com/kindle-books/food-storage-recommends/#spirulinapills
- Link 44: http://www.naturodoc.com/chlorella.htm
- Link 45: http://www.webmd.com/men/features/benefits-protein#1
- Link 46: https://rethinksurvival.com/kindle-books/food-storage-recommends/#proteinpowder
- Link 47: https://www.gnc.com/health-articles-tips/sports-performance/creatine-vs-protein-when-and-why.html
- Link 48: http://www.mayoclinic.org/healthy-lifestyle/nutrition-and-healthy-eating/multimedia/health-foods/sls-20076653?s=10
- Link 49: https://begoodorganics.com/blogs/subscribe

r-only-recipes/7991527-cacao-5-little-known-benefits-of-this-amazonian-superfood
- Link 50: https://rethinksurvival.com/kindle-books/food-storage-recommends/#nexabiotic
- Link 51: https://rethinksurvival.com/kindle-books/food-storage-recommends/#kefir
- Link 52: https://rethinksurvival.com/kindle-books/food-storage-recommends/#enzymes
- Link 53: https://www.webmd.com/diet/features/the-benefits-of-vitamin-c#1
- Link 54: https://rethinksurvival.com/kindle-books/food-storage-recommends/#vitaminc
- Link 55: https://draxe.com/psyllium-husk/
- Link 56: https://rethinksurvival.com/kindle-books/food-storage-recommends/#psyllium
- Link 57: http://www.lifehack.org/articles/lifestyle/11-benefits-of-green-tea-that-you-didnt-know-about.html
- Link 58: https://draxe.com/apple-cider-vinegar-uses/
- Link 59: https://www.organicfacts.net/health-benefits/oils/health-benefits-of-fish-oil.html
- Link 60: https://rethinksurvival.com/kindle-books/food-storage-recommends/#fishoil

- Link 61: https://www.healthline.com/health/food-nutrition/top-raw-honey-benefits#digestion-and-gut-health
- Link 62: https://www.sunfood.com/blog/newsletters/40-uses-for-honey-that-will-blow-your-socks-off/
- Link 63: https://www.healthline.com/nutrition/manuka-honey-uses-benefits
- Link 64: https://rethinksurvival.com/delicious-homemade-banana-bread/
- Link 65: https://www.webmd.com/food-recipes/features/food-synergy-nutrients-that-work-better-together#1
- Link 66: https://rethinksurvival.com/books/food-storage-share.htm
- Link 67: https://rethinksurvival.com/books/food-storage-checklist.php.
- Link 68: https://rethinksurvival.com/kindle-books/
- Link 69: https://rethinksurvival.com/kindle-books/survival-uses-book/
- Link 70: https://rethinksurvival.com/kindle-books/smartphone-survival-apps-book/

- Link 71: https://rethinksurvival.com/kindle-books/home-security-book/
- Link 72: https://rethinksurvival.com/kindle-books/diy-survival-projects-book/
- Link 73: https://rethinksurvival.com/kindle-books/bug-out-bag-book/
- Link 74: https://rethinksurvival.com/kindle-books/secret-hides-book/
- Link 75: https://rethinksurvival.com/kindle-books/earthquake-survival-book/
- Link 76: https://rethinksurvival.com/kindle-books/small-space-prepping-book/
- Link 77: https://rethinksurvival.com/kindle-books/pet-safety-plan-book/
- Link 78: https://rethinksurvival.com/kindle-books/survival-toolbox-book/
- Link 79: https://rethinksurvival.com/kindle-books/id-theft-book/
- Link 80: https://rethinksurvival.com/kindle-books/bug-out-bag-book/
- Link 81: https://rethinksurvival.com/books/food-storage-review.php

Made in the USA
Middletown, DE
27 October 2021

51067689R10080